TRANSFERRING PROFESSIONAL LEARNING

TRANSFERRING PROFESSIONAL LEARNING TO SCHOOLS IN A CARIBBEAN SETTING

Context and Culture Matter

Freddy James, Susan Herbert and Jennifer Yamin-Ali

The University of the West Indies Press
Mona • St Augustine • Cave Hill • Global • Five Islands

The University of the West Indies Press
7A Gibraltar Hall Road, Mona
Kingston 7, Jamaica
www.uwipress.com

© 2024, Freddy James, Susan Herbert and Jennifer Yamin-Ali

All rights reserved. Published 2024

A catalogue record of this book is available from the National Library of Jamaica.

ISBN: 978-976-640-956-2 (print)
ISBN: 978-976-640-957-9 (epub)

The University of the West Indies Press has no responsibility for the persistence or accuracy of URLs for external or third-party internet websites referred to in this publication and does not guarantee that any content on such websites is, or will remain, accurate or appropriate.

Cover Illustration by Carlene Jennifer Smith
Cover and text design by Christina Moore Fuller
Printed in the United States of America

CONTENTS

List of Tables and Figures ... *vii*

Preface ... *ix*

Acknowledgements ... *xv*

1. The Genesis ... 1

2. Transfer of Knowledge from the Learning Context to the Practice Context ... 33

3. Factors Facilitating the Transfer of Learning and Sustaining Effective Practice ... 75

4. Challenges to Sustaining Effective Practice Post Professional Learning ... 110

5. Contribution to School Development and Beyond ... 140

6. A Model for Sustaining Effective Practice ... 166

Index ... 183

List of Tables and Figures

Figure 1.1: Interplay among the Elements That Influence Transfer ... 7

Figure 6.1: Model for Sustaining Graduates' Effective Practice Post Professional Learning ... 171

Table 1.1: The Dimensions of School Culture ... 16

Preface

Imagine that you are an educator involved in the professional learning of teachers and school leaders for many years. Year after year, you hear various stakeholders comment that teachers and school leaders have completed the postgraduate Diploma in Education (DipEd) but are not practising what they have learnt. After hearing this for some time, the authors became determined to investigate why this statement was being made and what was happening to graduates' practice once they completed the DipEd. This book explores how teachers and school leaders transition from their learning to their practice context. It also explores their contributions to their institutions once their initial preparation programme ends. It provides evidence-based conclusions that indicate that school context and school culture influence the extent to which graduates promote and practise what they have learnt in their professional learning and development programme. A qualitative approach that employed a multi-site case study research design was used. Data collection methods included observations, document analysis and in-depth face-to-face interviews with practitioners in the field.

This book adds to the knowledge base about teacher education programmes and practitioners' realities. It argues that school context and school culture matter for teacher development and provides a collaborative model for teacher and school leader preparation. The book focuses on sustainability of practice of graduates of an in-service teacher education programme. It consists of six chapters: "The Genesis", "Transfer of Knowledge from the Learning Context to the Practice Context", "Factors Facilitating the Transfer of Learning and Sustaining Effective Practice", "Challenges to Sustaining Effective Practice Post Professional Learning", "Contribution to School Development and Beyond", and "A Model for Sustaining Effective Practice".

Why This Book? Why Now?

As significant changes in technology, climate, politics, health and socio-economics continue to occur within the global landscape, education and educators are being challenged to reconfigure and adjust to maintain cultural and contextual relevance. Professional learning programmes are required to make the adjustments to ensure that what is taught in the learning space is transferred to the practice space. This book offers an empirical evidence-based model that provides an original perspective on the conditions for sustaining graduates' effective practice post professional learning and development based on existing literature and the authors' own experiences. While the model was generated from data within the Trinidad and Tobago context, the conditions it proposes for sustaining graduates' practice post professional learning and development could be empirically tested and applied in other contexts. Thus, an undoubted merit of this book is that although the research was conducted in Trinidad and Tobago, its implications refer to fundamental issues currently impacting educators' professional learning and development in any location.

What Makes This Book Unique?

The book provides interactive segments. At the end of each case presented in the chapters, the authors' reflections are presented, and users are provided questions to further interrogate the issues raised within their own cultural and contextual education environment. In this way, the book becomes personalized. Many studies have been done on the impact of postgraduate studies on educators' practice. These studies tend to focus on the short-term impact of postgraduate studies and mainly on whether participants will use the skills and knowledge they have gained in their future practice. In contrast, the research presented in this book explores via an in-depth investigation the long-term impact of the DipEd programme on graduates' practice. Further, the research not only utilized interviews but also classroom observations, which significantly increases the credibility of its implications.

Organization of Chapters

Chapter 1: The Genesis

The introduction justifies an examination of how graduates function once they have left the initial preparation programme and continue to function at their schools. We present an exploration of literature related to context and theories of culture and introduce a description of the situational context of the research. A description of the methodology is provided. We also present our thesis that the degree to which educators transfer and sustain their knowledge gained while on a professional learning and development programme is determined by specific factors which are highlighted in chapter 3.

Chapter 2: Transfer of Knowledge from the Learning Context to the Practice Context

Chapter 2 focuses on the issue of graduates' practice, specifically how knowledge is transferred into instructional and pedagogical practice. It examines how practitioners in administration, foreign languages and science transferred the knowledge gained in the learning contexts to their practice contexts. The chapter begins with a discussion of the literature on knowledge transfer and then presents each participant's experiences as cases for each discipline.

Chapter 3: Factors Facilitating the Transfer of Learning and Sustaining Effective Practice

This chapter discusses the factors which facilitate the transfer of learning and sustaining effective practice once practitioners have completed their professional development preparation. The teachers' belief that the strategies that they have learned can work; their commitment to change; their efficacy; whether a culture of innovation exists within the practice environment; the students' interests and experiences; and the context of the practice environment are the factors identified as facilitating knowledge transfer and sustaining practice. Through the cases presented, the authors conclude that the key facilitating factors are school factors (resources, culture, school leadership), personal factors and external factors.

Chapter 4: Challenges to Sustaining Effective Practice Post Professional Learning

This chapter focuses on the challenges graduates of the programme faced as they experienced the reality of their classrooms post professional learning and development. Such challenges included external factors such as societal expectations of teachers and teaching, and systemic ones such as material and human resources, school and ministry promotion policies and school culture. Student culture, learning ability and socio-economic background also posed challenges to the graduates. In large part, a non-alignment between the realities of the education environment in which teachers functioned and what they had learned on the teacher education programme created obstacles in their attempts to develop and sustain effective practice. Some felt that the programme did not prepare them for the types of dire challenges they had to face in their teaching environment. Though many of their challenges appeared to be outside their control, at times they adjusted their dispositions by developing tools to cope. Yet there was evidence of frustration by their powerlessness to ameliorate their context and culture.

Chapter 5: Contribution to School Development and Beyond

Teachers' contribution to a school is indicative not only of their commitment to the school and their profession but also of their sense of belonging in the institution. This chapter explores the degree to which graduates contribute to their schools' and communities' development. It also discusses the nature and impact of their contributions. The chapter begins with a brief review of the theory of teacher contribution to school development and explains in detail the graduates' contributions to the development of their schools and communities. Selected contributions within the school context involved creating resources, presenting at professional development exercises, collaborating with others to conduct research and mentoring staff. External contributions included collaborating with the Ministry of Education to host professional development exercises for teachers and participating in community activities, such as competitions.

Chapter 6: A Model for Sustaining Effective Practice

Chapter 6 presents conclusions derived from a synthesis of the discussion of the findings from this research. These findings include the status of graduates' practice, the factors facilitating and inhibiting the transfer of knowledge, skills and competencies developed within the learning context and transferred to their school context, as well as graduates' contributions to school development. It presents a model, with evidence-based justifications, as a framework for sustaining effective practice. Components of the model include teachers' characteristics and dispositions and the nature of the professional development programme. A key feature of the model for sustaining effective practice is the role of the context and culture of the institution in which the graduates engage in professional practice. We posit that graduates of the programme are within a liminal space where there is the potential for transformation. The implication is that the school context and culture must provide a supportive environment which allows the seeds planted within the professional development programmes to flourish. We therefore argue that context and culture matter in any attempt at professional development that has sustaining effective practice as its goal.

Acknowledgements

We would like to thank all the committed educators who participated in the study for their insights and stories that made this work possible. We are grateful for their cooperation and for giving of their time so generously.

1. The Genesis

Introduction and Background

This book focuses on what graduates from an in-service 'initial' postgraduate teacher education programme do once they return to their schools and classrooms. The programme, titled the Diploma in Education (DipEd), is provided by the University of the West Indies, St Augustine, School of Education (UWISoE) to in-service secondary schoolteachers. In Trinidad and Tobago, professional certification is not mandatory for entry into the teaching service at the secondary level. The postgraduate DipEd programme was designed to provide initial formal professional preparation to practising teachers. It comprised four major components: the foundations of education, curriculum as process, project in the theory of education and the practice of education, and underpinned by sociocultural theories of learning, relied heavily on collaborative activities in all courses. At the time of this research, the programme lasted ten months.

There is little or no research, internationally, regionally or locally, on the factors that facilitate or inhibit professionally unprepared practitioners in transitioning to the status of being professionally prepared practitioners. Knowledge and understanding of the facilitating and inhibiting school contextual and cultural factors, as well as knowledge and understanding of the DipEd programme, are required to understand the environment that enables and sustains effective teaching practice. Yet the DipEd programme is often assessed in isolation from the education culture and context to which teachers return. In response to stakeholder perspectives, we initiated an investigation into the actions and behaviours of graduates from 2004 to 2009 within their respective environments. This investigation sought to understand both the factors that facilitate and inhibit the application of concepts educators were introduced to during the programme. Specifically, the researchers investigated the practice of participants who were enrolled in the science, foreign language and educational administration specializations in the 2004-9 programme. The research explored the extent to which the programme impacted the professional practice of these educators after they exited it. Specifically, the research focused on the degree to which the principles taught during their professional learning in the programme were incorporated into their day-to-day practice in their schools, as well as the perspectives of their heads of departments (HoDs) and principals.

The Relationship between Professional Learning, Development and Sustaining Practice

Darling-Hammond et al. (2009, 3) state as follows:

> In an effective professional learning system, school leaders learn from experts, mentors and their peers about how to become true instructional leaders. They work with staff members to create the culture, structures and dispositions for continuous professional learning and create pressure and support to help teachers continuously improve by better understanding students' needs, making data-driven decisions regarding content and pedagogy and assessing students' learning within a framework of high expectations.

The researchers accept this position on professional learning offered by Darling-Hammond et al. (2009) and used it to guide our understanding of professional learning. Further, we embrace Ken Jones's definition of professional learning, which requires the active participation of all involved, including teachers. Jones (2021, 2) states,

> '*Professional learning*' involves active learning; it is a continuing process; it focuses on enquiry, analysis, reflection, evaluation, further action; it should be professionally critical; in its best forms it is collaborative; and it enables an approach which is not confined to a linear interpretation of future events and ways of working...Crucially, the essence of professional learning focuses less on the qualities or deficits of teachers and more on the need to make a difference for learners...So to generate effective pupil learning we have to ensure purposeful *teacher learning* and then translate this into effective practice.

Still, achieving and sustaining purposeful teacher learning does not happen in a vacuum. There are conditions that must exist within schools' contexts and cultures that facilitate the necessary teacher transformation. Jones (2021, 2) notes the following: "To achieve and sustain this it is essential to have effective senior and middle leadership because without their intervention teacher change is likely to be ad hoc and individualistic and there is likely to be more rather than less variation within institutions".

Literature suggests that professional learning that leads to instructional changes should include four key elements. Firstly, it must focus on the interactions in the context of all aspects of the instructional space, such as teachers, students and the instructional materials. Secondly, there should be an alignment with the implementation of instruction and thirdly, time should be included for collaborative activities during the professional learning process. Fourthly, there is a considerable body of research that acknowledges the importance of the collaborative process in professional learning programmes and suggests that involving teachers and school leaders in research and inquiry within that process contributes to school and system improvement (Cordingley 2015; Campbell, Liberman and Yashkina 2016; Chapman et al. 2016; Harris and Jones 2017; James and Figaro-Henry 2017). Notwithstanding the importance of these elements, equally important to the success of the transfer is the context in which the interaction occurs since each school and classroom has its unique environment (Cohen and Ball 1999; Hopkins 2001; Chapman 2005; Thrupp and Lupton 2006; Harris and Chrispeels 2006; Darling-Hammond et al. 2009). We acknowledge that a necessary component of developing and sustaining educators' expertise is grounding professional learning in ongoing practice (Putnam and Borko 2000).

The current in-service postgraduate diploma in education programme offered at UWISoE has all these elements. The courses that focus on educational foundations, pedagogy and action research all contribute to the "practicum" component of the programme, which takes place within the educators' school and classroom contexts. Students are encouraged to implement new concepts and strategies introduced in the programme, and their supervisors and peers observe them as they teach and conduct clinical supervision, in the case of the educational administration students. The practicum also allows for collaboration and meaningful discussions between supervisors, other colleagues in the programme and colleagues in their schools. Additionally, this component establishes networks of educators who can support each other's ongoing practice through discourse and sharing materials and practices they have found workable in their contexts.

The Concept of Sustainability

The assumption underpinning education and training programmes is that the ideas, concepts and principles promoted are worthwhile and are relevant to the participants' context of practice. It is generally expected that the knowledge, competencies, skills and dispositions developed will be useful to participants and will be utilized in the work environment continuously, that is, that the new practices will be sustained. Sustainability is often defined in terms of maintenance or perpetuation and fostering of the practice (Paris 2012) or as a continuation beyond efforts of initiation (Southcott and McCrone 2011). The definitions above imply a focus on, and implementation of, ideas and actions deemed necessary for improvement. However, other writers focus their concept of sustainability not on actions or current thinking but on the desire for improvement. Fullan, in 2004, puts forth a systems perspective defining sustainability as "the capacity of a system to engage in the complexities of continuous improvement" (quoted in Katz, Earl and Ben Jaafar 2009, 104). In addition, Hargreaves and Fink (2005) (quoted in Katz, Earl and Ben Jaafar 2009) emphasize the role of leadership and the learning dimension and define it as "leadership and improvement [that] preserves and develops deep learning for all that spreads and lasts". Thus, sustainability means more than whether something lasts. It implies that groups continually learn from their experiences with the change and continue to develop capacity in what they are attempting to change (James and Figaro-Henry 2017). Within this experience of change, one finds that graduates of a teacher education programme operating within a changing system may need to adapt their own teaching philosophy as they come to a new understanding of their professional community (Yamin-Ali 2014). "This approach to sustainability means that change is part of the individual's and group's way of working – it is a taken-for-granted part of how they think and act, as they continually strive to build capacity to support student learning. Sustainability is not conformity and the dogged pursuit of some mandate. It is grounded in sustaining improvement, not particular actions" (Katz, Earl and Ben Jaafar 2009, 104).

Although desirable, it is recognized that sustainability outcomes are not often realized in practice, and researchers have investigated two sides of the issue – the nature and characteristics of the education/training programme and the nature and characteristics of the contexts of practice to facilitate or hinder sustainability. With regard to the former, it is acknowledged that one-shot workshop-type activities do not have a good record for transfer into the work environment due to insufficient time to achieve change and buy-in by addressing participants' deeply held beliefs. For example, the programme should allow for the interrogation of participants' beliefs about the expected change and opportunities for ownership of the strategies suggested (Melnyk et al. 2011). With regard to the nature of the practice context, the following are characteristics of the work environment required to sustain the application of knowledge and skills: leadership and champions and mentors (Boyd, Szplit and Zbróg 2014; Kain 2003; Melnyk et al. 2011); development of professional learning communities referred to earlier by Katz, Earl and Ben Jaafar (2009) as communities of practice; policy, for example, organizational policies (Melnyk et al. 2011, 57); and continued high-quality learning experiences. Heckman in 2008 (quoted in Darling-Hammond 2010, 35) notes, "the advantages gained from effective early interventions are best sustained when they are followed by continued high quality learning experiences", cultural factors and individual as well as organizational change (Melnyk et al. 2011). Additionally, with regard to sustaining academic-practice partnerships, Breslin et al. (2011, 33) found that (a) change is inevitable, (b) leadership matters at all levels, (c) succession planning is essential, (d) persistence toward established goals is necessary and (e) relationships are the glue to sustain forward movement.

These definitions and ideas about sustainability provided the lens through which to interpret observations of graduates' practice and their perspectives on sustaining change initiated during their professional learning programme. They also served as the lens for interpreting the perspectives of the heads of departments (HoDs) and principals.

Positionality

Our thesis is that the degree to which educators transfer and sustain their knowledge gained while on a professional learning programme is determined by: teachers' belief that the strategies that they have learned can work; their commitment to change; their efficacy; whether a culture of innovation exists within the practice environment; students' interests and experiences; and the context of the practice environment. Thus, the degree to which educators transfer knowledge to their practice is determined first by the content and delivery of the programme and then by the school context. If the participants feel motivated and empowered by the principles they learn in the programme and perceive their value, they are more likely to transfer this knowledge to their practice. Conversely, if they think there is little or no value in what they are learning during the programme, the likelihood of knowledge transfer reduces. Therefore, an interplay of various elements determines whether educators transfer knowledge from a professional learning space to their practice space and the degree of such transfer. These elements are the individual educator, the 'instructional triangle' (Cohen and Ball 1999), the context of practice and the nature and delivery of the professional learning itself. These are depicted in figure 1.1 below, while deeper expositions of the elements follow.

Figure 1.1: Interplay among the Elements That Influence Transfer

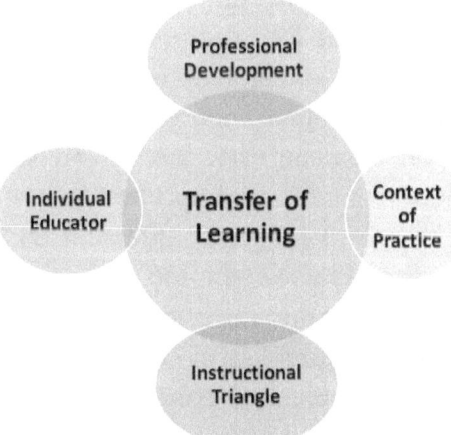

The Issue of Transfer

Schwartz, Bransford and Sears (2005, 7) contend that expanding the classic definition of transfer to include "flexible adaptation of old responses to new settings" is still too restrictive for exploring issues of transfer. They consider that instead of focusing on the direct application of learning to new situations, teacher preparation should focus on preparation for future learning. Teacher education programmes need to include transfer in conceptualizing programme content and approach. Spiro et al. (1995) believe that cognitive flexibility is achieved once one can successfully transfer learning. Cognitive flexibility theory focuses on the nature of learning in complex and "imperfect" settings. Spiro and Jehng (1990, 165) define cognitive flexibility as "the ability to spontaneously restructure one's knowledge in adaptive response to radically changing situational demands".

The cognitive flexibility theory has implications for teacher education programmes and how they prepare teachers for effective practice because it emphasizes the presentation of information from multiple perspectives and the presentation of varied examples using several case studies. The theory also stresses that effective learning is context-dependent, so instruction needs to be contextualized. Constructed knowledge is most important in the learning process. To ensure students' adequate learning, it is imperative to offer them opportunities to construct their own representations of information.

Refocusing on elements that have been seen as core to teacher education content, the important role of reflection on practice must be considered in the quest for the sustainability of effective practice. As we attempt to move teachers along the continuum from "the apprenticeship of observation" (Lortie 1975) to overcome "the problem of enactment" (Kennedy 1999) whilst facing "the problem of complexity" (Hammerness et al. 2005, 359), teacher education programmes must enable student teachers "to develop metacognitive habits of mind that can guide decisions and reflection on practice in support of continual improvement" (Hammerness et al. 2005, 359).

To be effective and to promote the transfer of learning, teacher education programmes must contextualize their content. If not, what is learned will remain abstract and not applied. Herbert, Yamin-Ali and James's (2018) study on transitioning from the professional learning environment to the practice environment found that there was some evidence of transfer from the learning to the practice context. That study supports the view that content needs to be presented in authentic settings and situations that would normally involve that knowledge. In such situated learning, learners become part of a "community of practice" and begin to embody certain beliefs and behaviours common to that community. This also has relevance for professional learning which addresses specific professional needs of either novice or experienced teachers. Situated learning becomes supremely necessary in order to complement the initial teacher education (ITE) professional preparation for teachers. Context becomes a key issue when we consider the observation by Barras et al. (2016) that issues such as the perceived disconnectedness between foundations courses and the reality of teachers' experiences; the disconnect between the reality of the teachers' working world and the world of the institutions of teacher preparation; and the fit between teacher preparation programmes and the design of the field experience, as well as the very content of teacher education programmes, negatively impact the effectiveness of ITEs. They contend that these issues are all interrelated and affect teachers' ability to transform their practices and transfer learning from teacher education programmes into their classrooms.

The sustainability of effective practice is clearly predicated on adequate preparation on the one hand. However, in tandem with initial preparation, teachers must become lifelong learners. "Adult education and training can help individuals to upskill and re-skill over time, to ensure their skills remain relevant in an ever-changing world. It is important even for countries with highly skilled populations to continue enacting policies that promote lifelong learning and raise participation and motivation" (OECD 2019, 77).

Conceptions of what lifelong learning entails vary. Fundamentally, it can include both self-directed and systemically driven efforts. According to Coolahan (2002, 13):

> ...it is only intelligent, highly skilled, imaginative, caring and well-educated teachers who will be able to respond satisfactorily to the demands placed on the education system in developed societies. If society's concern is to improve quality in education and to foster creative, enterprising, innovative, self-reliant young people, with the capacity and motivation to go on as lifelong learners, then this will not happen unless the corps of teachers are themselves challenging, innovative and lifelong learners.

As we recognize that teachers' roles in the future will augment and morph, the necessary related knowledge and skills base would require teachers to engage in professional and personal development on an ongoing basis, as lifelong learners (Burke 2002; Good, Biddle and Godson 1997).

Individual Educators

Cohen and Ball (1999, 3) state as follows:

> Teachers' intellectual and personal resources influence instructional interactions by shaping how teachers apprehend, interpret, and respond to materials and students. There is considerable evidence that teachers vary in their ability to notice, interpret, and adapt to differences among students. Important teacher resources in this connection include their conceptions of knowledge, understanding of content, and flexibility of understanding; acquaintance with students' knowledge and ability to relate to, interact with, and learn about students; and their repertoire of means to represent and extend knowledge, and to establish classroom environments.

Other researchers stress the importance of educators' ability to collaborate with others by creating professional learning communities as a lever that facilitates the transfer and sustainability of practice (Louis and Marks 1998; Wenger 1998; McLaughlin and Talbert 2006; Stoll and Louis 2007; Timperley et al. 2007; Vescio, Ross and Adams 2008; Pang and Wang 2016). Wenger (1998, 85) notes: "…as a locus of engagement in action, interpersonal relationships, shared knowledge, and negotiation of enterprises, such communities hold the key to real transformation – the kind that has real effect on people's lives… The influence of other forces (e.g., the control of an institution or the authority of an individual) are no less important, but… they are mediated by the communities in which their meanings are negotiated in practice".

Professional learning communities are not solely for the purpose of formal learning but may provide learning that is difficult to capture or document but exceedingly significant, nonetheless. That is, the learning from modelling, whether through instituted or informal mentors, can be a powerful channel of inspiration and empowerment for the positive transformation of educators (Yamin-Ali 2021).

Instructional Triangle

According to Cohen and Ball (1999), the instructional triangle relates to the interactions among teachers, instructional material and technologies and the students within a particular context. Cohen and Ball (1999, 3) posit that it is not each individual element within the triangle that brings about learning but the interaction of these elements within a particular context. They further explain how each of these individual elements influences the interaction within the instructional triangle. They state that, for example:

> Teachers' intellectual and personal resources influence instructional interactions by shaping how teachers apprehend, interpret, and respond to materials and students. There is considerable evidence that teachers vary in their ability to notice, interpret, and adapt to differences among students.

Important teacher resources in this connection include their conceptions of knowledge, understanding of content, and flexibility of understanding; acquaintance with students' knowledge and ability to relate to, interact with, and learn about students; and their repertoire of means to represent and extend knowledge, and to establish classroom environments.

Cohen and Ball (1999, 3-4) state that "students bring experience, prior knowledge, and habits of mind, and these influence how they apprehend, interpret, and respond to materials and teachers". Thus, the way a lesson might unfold, using particular problems in one class, might be quite different from another class. Additionally, they claim that "instructional materials can mediate students' engagement with the content to be learned, though sometimes the materials themselves are what is to be learned. They can be thought of as the material (as opposed to social) technologies of instruction, including print, video, and computer-based multimedia" (4).

Context of Practice

The concept of context is examined at various levels: the schools, community and country. There are differences in terms of what is considered at the different contextual levels. The country context might relate to factors about the state of development of the country – whether the country is developed, underdeveloped or developing and the socio-economic conditions associated with it. For the purpose of this book, the school's context is the sum of the internal and external factors that characterize the environment and framework within which it is situated. Some of these factors have physical attributes. For example, the type of homes in the community, whether the community is rural or urban in nature and the physical landscape. West and Ainscow (2006, 4) describe these variables as "ingredients", and argue that a suitable way forward to improve student achievement in schools is "to focus on determining the right sort of 'ingredients' mixed to suit the contexts and circumstances of individual schools". Some of these "ingredients" are ethereal, and these relate to the people, within the contexts, their practices, attitudes, customs and interactions, in other words, their culture. It is in this way that the concepts of culture and context converge.

Schools should not be viewed as a homogeneous group. Rather, the singularity of each school should be recognized so that the focus of improvement is based on the specific contextual factors existing within a particular school at a particular point in time (Thrupp and Lupton 2006; Harris and Chrispeels 2006; Chapman 2005; Hopkins 2001; Dalin 1994). According to Thrupp and Lupton (2006), an understanding of context can help policymakers make adequate and effective educational provisions to increase student achievement.

The Nature and Delivery of the Professional Learning

Models of Teacher Education

A pre-service model ensures that teachers enter the classroom already equipped to fulfil their roles in the teaching community. Even though their ITE experience would include temporary classroom experiences, they bring little experience of teaching and learning to bear on their professional learning, except for their own experiences as students in the school system. Despite this, teachers intend for their students to benefit from a practice that reflects professionally appropriate knowledge, competencies and dispositions.

On the other hand, in-service ITE offers a pathway to a more constructivist approach to professional learning in that teachers in this scenario have already been situated in the classroom and bring to bear their prior and current experiences and knowledge as they interact with new programme content. Through varying modes, they have also benefited from prior learning through "learning-on-the go", mentors and observation. As practising teachers, it is also likely that they would have had the advantage of training opportunities provided by their ministries of education or other governmental bodies.

ITE could be offered using a concurrent or consecutive model. In the concurrent model, prospective teachers enrol in a four- or five-year degree in their subject specialization and an education degree or diploma. In the consecutive model, prospective teachers earn their teaching qualification full-time in one year after their bachelor's or master's degree. In some instances, there are alternative pathways to ITE. In Trinidad and Tobago, historically, ITE for secondary teachers has followed an in-service model via government-funded scholarships.

The Issue of Quality

Regardless of the model of teacher preparation, the issue of quality arises as one that determines the ultimate outcome of any teacher education initiative. We submit that quality does not simply mean maintaining standards for the professional learning programme but ensuring that there is alignment between educators' preparation, practice and the intended outcomes of education. Therefore, educators must be adequately equipped to meet the needs of twenty-first-century learners, and this underscores a need for intentional professional learning. Critical thinking, problem-solving, creativity, metacognition, communication, digital and technological literacy, civic responsibility and global awareness are the identified skills and competencies for twenty-first-century learners (Dede 2010; Schleicher 2012). Twenty-first-century educators must prepare students for jobs in the future and prepare them to solve cultural and social problems that do not yet exist (Goodwin 2015). According to Clementi and Terrill (2013, 2), "learners need to develop real-world skills they can use throughout their work, career, and personal lives".

Programmes are one benchmark used by nations to attempt to ensure quality standards for teacher education. With regard to quality assurance at the early childhood to secondary levels, in the United States, the Teacher Education Accreditation Council (TEAC) and the National Council for Accreditation of Teacher Education (NCATE) have brought the educational accreditation rules under one agency known as the Council for the Accreditation of Educational Preparation (CAEP). Their mission is to advance equity and excellence in educator preparation through evidence-based accreditation that assures quality and supports continuous improvement to strengthen student learning. In Europe, the European Association for Quality Assurance in Higher Education (ENQA) has played a significant role in establishing standards and guidelines for quality assurance in higher education. ENQA expects that institutions should have a policy and associated procedures for the assurance of the quality and standards of their programmes and awards and that they should themselves be explicitly committed to the development of a culture that recognizes the importance of quality and quality assurance in their work (De Coster, Forsthuber and Steinberger 2006). Within the Caribbean context, standards for teachers and school leaders have been created and ratified by the Caribbean Community (CARICOM), although these standards are yet to be implemented across the region. In Trinidad and Tobago, Higher Education Institutions (HEIs) assure quality through their accreditation body, the Accreditation Council of Trinidad and Tobago (ACTT). Therefore, the quality of the DipEd is assured through the approval granted to the University of the West Indies (UWI) through the ACTT. Additionally, internally, UWI's quality policy requires a five-year cycle of review of programmes in all departments.

In addition to the four key elements elucidated above, other factors that relate to the transfer of practice are discussed below.

Theories of Culture

Theories of educational and organizational culture fall into various frames. There is the "anthropological" (Deal and

Peterson 1999; Deal and Kennedy 1982; 1983), which focuses on the customs and rituals that societies develop over the course of their history. There is also the "situational", for example, "the way we do things around here" (Deal and Kennedy 1982). Another approach is the "shared meanings or group culture", which Schein (1992, 12) refers to as "a pattern of shared basic assumptions that the group learned as it solved its problems of external adaptation and internal integration that has worked well enough to be considered valid and, therefore, to be taught to new members as the correct way to perceive, think, and feel in relation to those problems".

There is yet another frame, described as "the subterranean aspect of school culture", whereby culture is referred to as the micro-politics of organizations (Prosser 1999; Stoll 1999; Hoyle 1986). The micro-political perspective recognizes that formal structures within organizations could be easily subverted by the powerful informal structures which consist, for example, of group affiliations and cliques. Angelides and Ainscow (2000) proposed a framework for analysing "critical incidents" to gain a deeper understanding of the concept of school culture as it impacts individual schools' assumptions, practices and relationships. More recently, Schoen and Teddlie (2008, 139–40) have provided a new integrated model of school culture, which is useful as it incorporates, to some extent, the extant models.

Table 1.1: The Dimensions of School Culture

I. **Professional Orientation** The activities and attitudes that characterize the degree of professionalism present in the faculty	II. **Organizational Structure** The style of leadership, communication and processes that characterize the way school conducts its business
III. **Quality of the Learning Environment** The intellectual merit of activities in which students are typically engaged	IV. **Student-centred Focus** The collective efforts and programmes offered to support student achievement

Source: Schoen and Teddlie (2008, 138–40)

The model describes school culture as comprising four elements: (i) professional orientation, (ii) organizational structure, (iii) quality of the learning environment and (iv) student-centred focus, which are explained in table 1.1.

In addition to drawing on Schoen and Teddlie's (2008) model for conceptual clarity, this chapter also draws on Prosser's (1999) categorization of culture, which is useful as it relies more on clarifying the meaning of culture within the context of its use, rather than relying merely on its definition. Prosser identified four broad categories of culture applicable to schools. There is the "wider culture", which emphasizes the relationship between the national culture/s and that of the school and recognizes that the two impact and influence each other. "Generic culture" reflects the similarities that may exist between and among schools. "Unique culture" relates to the predominant values embraced by a school that establishes the guiding policies and mores for it. This is what distinguishes one school of similar type from another. Finally, "perceived culture" that encompasses "on-site perceived culture" describes the staff and casual visitors' views of the school, reflective of elements of its unique culture. "Off-site perceived culture" describes the outsiders' "view of a school" (Prosser 1999, 7-8).

Culture is not a static phenomenon, therefore. The culture of a school can change as it adjusts and adapts to changing circumstances within the internal or external environment. Culture underpins and can undermine every aspect of a school's development, especially regarding classroom practices (Harris 2002; Hopkins 2001; Fullan and Stiegelbauer 1991). Therefore, schools should deliberately and carefully transact and create cultures by taking cognizance of their goals, vision, environment and community within which the school is situated.

Sustaining Effective Practice

Within the literature, a number of terms, such as continuing professional learning, continuous professional development and continuing professional development, are used to describe formal in-service programmes, as well as workshops geared to up-skilling educators and capacity building. This study uses the term professional learning, except where there is a direct quotation in which any of the other terms are used. It is acknowledged that a key element of teacher professionalism is continuing professional learning (CPL) (OECD 2019; Ingersoll et al. 2018; Darling-Hammond et al. 2017; Dias-Lacy and Guirguis 2017; Opfer and Pedder 2011). Therefore, pre- and in-service ITE does not preclude the need for CPL. Therefore, ITE should ideally be planned along with a national policy for teacher licensure in which CPL would play a major role. According to Darling-Hammond et al. (2017), the highest-performing systems in the world provide regular "professional development", which is closely aligned with their teaching. They further explain that continuous learning is provided through "incentives and infrastructure for [teacher] learning; time and opportunity for collaboration; curriculum development and lesson study; teacher research; teacher-led PD; appraisal and feedback" (Darling-Hammond et al. 2017, 15).

It is critical to consider the challenges of "teaching effectively in an imperfect world" (Hammerness et al. 2005, 365) in order to comprehend the goal of sustaining effective practice post-institutionalized teacher preparation. In a discussion among teacher educators and school professionals to identify potential gaps in a teacher education programme in Seattle, participants recognized that practitioners regularly encounter constraints as a natural aspect of their professional lives. Consequently, it was emphasized that understanding the nature of these constraints is essential for practitioners to address them creatively (Hammerness et al. 2005).

Such constraints are magnified when teacher education programmes are not aligned with the reality of the context and culture of the teacher's professional setting. Darling-Hammond and Hammerness (2005) comment that according to research, the philosophy and practice of one's teacher education programme, if not aligned with that of one's school, could pose difficulties for the practising teacher. Feiman-Nemser and Buchman in 1985 (quoted in Darling-Hammond and Hammerness 2005) refer to this misalignment as the *two-worlds pitfall*. They comment, "Student teachers already in a difficult position of little authority and status in the classroom cannot easily overcome the disconnect between the ideas about teaching and learning espoused in their program and those they encounter in the classroom – leaving them feeling confused, guilty, and discouraged about their ability to be successful teachers."

Bransford et al. (2005) suggest there are two approaches to coping with misalignment. Both are efficient but in different ways. They explore the concepts of *routine expertise* and *adaptive expertise* in practice. They explain there is a distinct difference between routine experts and adaptive experts. The former are equipped with a set of core competencies that they continually use throughout their professional trajectory with increasing efficiency, whereas the latter expand the breadth and depth of their expertise by changing their core ideas, beliefs and competencies. Adaptive experts may experience some degree of dissonance initially as they move out of the comfort zone of what they were taught technically. However, the US NRC (2000) refers to this type of expertise as the "gold standard for learning", according to Bransford et al. (2005, 49). In terms of the goal of sustaining effective practice, whereas efficiency might be a desirable target in teaching, it might be bound to routine situations and contexts. Schwartz, Bransford and Sears (2005, 29) point out, though, that in order to transfer learning, we need to "teach for it". They advise that "transfer problems essentially disappear if we teach in contexts where people need to perform, and if we arrange experiences and environments so that the correct behaviors are driven by the environment".

Teacher Support

Teachers do need support in their continuing professional learning. The leadership literature in the field underscores the notion that leadership is the most important element of an effective school (Sergiovanni 1984; Elmore 2000; Stoll and Bolam 2004). According to Hirsh (2009, 3), schools "with the support of school systems and state departments of education need to make sure that professional learning is planned and organized to engage all teachers regularly and to benefit all students". Hirsh (2009) further iterates that the characteristics of such a system include high-quality, sustained professional learning throughout the school year, true instructional leadership, the cultural structures and dispositions for professional learning and regular scheduled meetings of learning teams. Most importantly, successful school-level professional learning systems are supported by national policy.

The view that school leadership is instrumental in ensuring that effective teaching is sustained in a school is supported by the Australian Department of Education & Training (DET) (Australia Victoria DET 2005, 7). They suggest that it is the responsibility of the effective school leader "to provide organisational conditions that are conducive for teachers to continuously improve their teaching practice by providing encouragement and fostering an environment that values sharing, trust, risk-taking, experimentation, collaborative inquiry and self-assessment". In addition, "they facilitate opportunities for staff to learn from each other, provide access to specialised knowledge and model continuous learning in their own practice".

The significant role and nature of a learning community are also highlighted by the Australian DET (Australia Victoria DET 2005, 8). They see it as a contributor to the development of both the school and the school community. Sharing to achieve the community's goals and vision is fundamental while valuing diversity, thus encouraging dissent and debate as opportunities for learning and growth. "Tradition and the 'way we do it here' attitudes are challenged and discussed, leading to new understandings, insights and practices."

New understandings through collaboration and community-oriented practice need to move from the insular to the far-reaching in order to best realize effective practices, including innovation and change. Zehetmeier (2010) suggests that to foster sustainability, not only at the individual (teacher's) level but also at the organizational (school's) level, Fullan's (2006) type of leadership is needed, one that "needs to go beyond the successes of increasing student achievement and move toward leading organizations to sustainability" (quoted in Zehetmeier 2010, 1956). He proposes Fullan's idea which states that sustainability stands a better chance if "'system thinkers' ... widen their sphere of engagement by interacting with other schools" and engage in "capacity-building through networks" (quoted in Zehetmeier 2010, 1956). "System thinkers" ought to also consider the issue of getting value for money in terms of the cost of teacher preparation programmes. Cilliers et al. (2020) highlight the positive role of a spillover impact from graduates into wider pools of beneficiaries who are their peers.

Notwithstanding the foregoing discussion on the sustainability of effective practice, it might be worthy to note the conclusion of work by Timperley et al. (2007), which sought to provide a first synthesis of research into the processes by which professional learning comes to impact student learning. A major finding of this synthesis has been that teachers need to have time and opportunity to engage with key ideas and integrate those ideas into a coherent theory of practice. Changing teaching practices in ways that have a significant impact on student outcomes is not easy. Policy and organizational contexts that continually shift priorities to the "next big thing", with little understanding/evaluation of how current practice is impacting desired outcomes for students, undermine the sustainability of changes already underway. Innovation needs to be carefully balanced with consolidation if professional learning experiences are to positively impact student outcomes. This innovation must also consider how to increase teachers' ability to utilize student-centred methodologies to foster student empowerment by improving their "capacity to act or exert themselves into their learning" (Sheninger and Murray 2017, 76).

Methodology

We adopted a qualitative approach for this research, which was designed as a multi-case study of selected graduates from the period 2004–9 in two curriculum areas: science and foreign language, as well as graduates from the specialization in educational administration. Each case of science, foreign language and educational administration was designed as a multi-site case study.

The researcher who currently serves as a lecturer/tutor in the respective specialization and who had served as each graduate's tutor in each specialization contacted by telephone five graduates who had scored a grade A or B+ in practice, spanning the period 2004–9. We introduced the project concept to them and requested their participation. Eleven of the fifteen graduates agreed to be involved in the field research of this multiple-case study. In essence, each case represents the teaching/practice of the selected discipline: foreign languages, science and educational administration. The cases are bounded by the practice of the discipline within the teachers' school contexts during the period 2014–15.

This research sought to answer the following research questions:
  a. How is knowledge transfer manifested in DipEd graduates' practice?
  b. What are the factors that facilitate the application and use of theories and principles introduced in the programme?

c. What factors inhibit the application and use of theories and principles introduced in the programme?
d. How do graduates contribute to school development?

Gaining Entry

The research team made a request to the Ministry of Education for permission to enter schools and to engage in the research, and in the case of Tobago, to the Tobago House of Assembly. We received permission before making any contact with the selected graduates and their principals. The relevant researcher scheduled school visits to each of the selected graduates who had agreed to participate on mutually convenient dates and times. We presented the letter of permission to both the teacher and principal before beginning the school visits. During the first school visit, we provided additional details about the research – the background, purpose and the data collection strategies.

The Participants

Eleven graduates agreed to participate in the research as follows: education administration (3), foreign languages (4) and science (4). The eleven principals of the schools in which the graduates were included agreed to participate. In addition, four heads of departments and two deans were interviewed. Thus, in total, there were twenty-eight participants from whom data were collected.

Data Collection

Data collection comprised classroom observations and individual semi-structured interviews with each graduate, as well as interviews with the principal of the school, the head of department (HoD) and the dean where available. However, data collection for the educational administration cases did not include classroom observation.

We collected classroom observation data from at least two class sessions per teacher, utilizing the same framework that was used to assess classroom practice during the 2004-9 programme period. That assessment framework organizes lesson presentation skills into three phases:

- pre-active, which assesses diagnostic and planning competence
- active, which assesses implementation competence and comprises motivational skills, questioning skills, communicative skills, classroom management and organizational skills, and closure skills, as well as teachers' use of group work, the teacher/learner relationships and instructional methods
- post-active, comprising assessment competence and continuity

In addition, we collected lesson plans and other relevant documents, such as schemes of work and clinical supervision reports, if available. Each researcher generated field notes. We used a pre-set interview protocol for the interviews with the principals, teachers, HoDs and deans. We audiotaped and transcribed those interviews. We also asked principals to complete and return an instrument, which requested supplementary data about the school context, such as school size, number of staff and their level of participation and interest in the DipEd programme, and overall student socio-economic status and performance. We also requested any additional documents that would assist in understanding the school context and culture.

Data Analysis

Each researcher analysed their respective cases. For the curriculum areas, we identified the lesson components and coded them in accordance with the competencies identified in the assessment framework. We assessed the classroom sessions, both in terms of the evidence of skills outlined in the assessment framework, as well as the extent to which these skills were employed effectively/competently. We identified patterns and themes. Regarding interview data, we analysed the interview transcripts from each participant inductively. That is, we read them line by line and subjected them to open coding and data aggregation (Creswell 2014) from which categories and themes emerged. We compared categories and themes to discern similarities between the graduate's perspectives and those of the school administration (principal, HoD and dean). We engaged in within-case analysis to identify similarities and differences among the cases. At this stage, each researcher reviewed the analysis of her colleagues to ensure that the themes suggested were supported by the participants' perspectives as revealed in the interviews. We made changes and modifications as required and, subsequently, discussed the emergent categories and themes deductively through the lens of Schoen and Teddlie's (2008) model of school culture and Prosser's (1999) micropolitical approach. Finally, the researchers collaborated on a cross-case analysis to identify the similarities and differences among the three.

Ethical Issues

We informed participants about the background and the purpose of the research during the first visit to their school. We also guaranteed them anonymity of reporting and formally acknowledged their right to withdraw from the research. We scheduled visits to the school for observations and interviews by appointment at the participants' convenience. We employed member-checking strategies by sharing researchers' interpretations of responses to interview questions, allowing for clarification as required.

In the following chapters, we share the participants' stories of their experience post-practice through identified themes. We have used pseudonyms in each instance to maintain the anonymity of the participants and their schools. The authors reported these cases in relation to their subject areas, at one level and at another level, within themes drawn from the research questions. Additionally, within each themed section, the authors sought to tell the story of each participant and compare their stories as they related their experiences within each theme. In this way, the authors captured some of the nuanced contextual and cultural differences that influence the experiences of the educators at each school. As such, in reporting the findings of the research, we constructed and created stories.

References

Ainscow, Mel, and Mel West, eds. 2006. *Improving Urban Schools: Leadership and Collaboration*. Berkshire, UK: Open University Press.

Angelides, Panayiotis, and Mel Ainscow. 2000. "Making Sense of the Role of Culture in School Improvement." *School Effectiveness and School Improvement* 11 (2): 145–63.

Australia Victoria DET (Department of Education & Training). 2005. *Professional Learning in Effective Schools: The Seven Principles of Highly Effective Professional Learning*. Melbourne: Victoria Department of Education & Training. https:// www.education .vic.gov.au/Documents/school/teachers/ profdev/proflearningeffectivesch.pdf.

Barras, Dyann, Benignus Bitu, Stephen Geofroy, S. Lochan, Lystra McLeod, and Shahiba Ali. 2016. "Social Science Teachers' Perceptions of Transformatory Learnings and the Transfer of Transformatory Learnings from an In-Service Professional Development Programme at The University of the West Indies, Trinidad and Tobago, 2013–2014." *Caribbean Curriculum* 24:75–99.

Boyd, Pete, Agnieszka Szplit, and Zuzanna Zbróg. 2014. Introduction to *Teacher Educators and Teachers as Learners: International Perspectives*, edited by Pete Boyd, Agnieszka Szplit, and Zuzanna Zbróg, 7–17. Kraków: Libron.

Bransford, John, Sharon Derry, David Charles Berliner, Karen Hammerness, and Kelly Ann Beckett. 2005. "Theories of Learning and Their Roles in Teaching." In *Preparing Teachers for a Changing World: What Teachers Should Learn and Be Able to Do*, edited by Linda Darling-Hammond and John Bransford, 40–87. San Francisco, CA: Jossey-Bass.

Breslin, Eileen, Mary Stefl, Suzanne Yarbrough, Dianne Frazor, Katherine Bullard, Kathy Light, Mickey Parsons, and Ashley Lowe. 2011. "Creating and Sustaining Academic-Practice Partnerships: Lessons Learned." *Journal of Professional Nursing* 27 (6): e33–e40.

Burke, Gerald. 2002. "Financing Lifelong Learning for All: An International Perspective." Working Paper No. 46. Centre for the Economics of Education and Training (CEET), Monash University, Victoria, Australia.

Campbell, Carol, Ann Lieberman, and Anna Yashkina. 2016. "Developing Professional Capital in Policy and Practice: Ontario's Teacher Learning and Leadership Program." *Journal of Professional Capital and Community* 1 (3): 219–36. https://doi.org/10.1108/JPCC-03-2016-0004.

Chapman, Christopher. 2005. *Improving Schools through External Intervention*. London: Continuum.

———. Hannah Chesnutt, Niamh Friel, Stuart Hall, and Kevin Lowden. 2016. "Professional Capital and Collaborative Inquiry Networks for Educational Equity and Improvement?" *Journal of Professional Capital and Community* 1 (3): 178–97.

Cohen, David K., and Deborah Loewenberg Ball. 1999. *Instruction, Capacity, and Improvement*. CPRE Research Report Series RR-43. Philadelphia, PA: Consortium for Policy Research in Education, University of Pennsylvania Graduate School of Education.

Cilliers, Jacobus, Brahm Fleisch, Janeli Kotzé, Mpumi Mohohlwane, and Stephen Taylor. 2020. "The Challenge of Sustaining Effective Teaching: Spillovers, Fade-Out, and the Cost-Effectiveness of Teacher Development Programs." Working paper. Department of Basic Education, Pretoria, South Africa. https://custom.cvent.com/4E741122FD8B4A1B97E483EC8BB51CC4/files/thechallengeofsustainingeffectiveteachingwithteaching with appendix.pdf.

Clementi, Donna, and Laura Terrill. 2013. *The Keys to Planning for Learning: Effective, Unit, and Lesson Design*. 2nd ed. Alexandria, VA: American Council on Teaching of Foreign Languages (ACTFL).

Cordingley, Philippa. 2015. "The Contribution of Research to Teachers' Professional Learning and Development." *Oxford Review of Education* 41 (2): 234–52.

Coolahan, John. 2002. "Teacher Education and the Teaching Career in an Era of Lifelong Learning." OECD Education Working Paper No. 2. OECD Publishing, Paris. https:doi.org/10.1787/19939019.

Creswell, John W. 2014. *Research Design: Qualitative, Quantitative and Mixed Methods Approaches*. 4th ed. Thousand Oaks, CA: SAGE.

Dalin, Per. 1994. *How Schools Improve: An International Report*. New York: Cassell.

Darling-Hammond, Linda. 2010. *The Flat World and Education: How America's Commitment to Equity Will Determine Our Future*. New York: Teachers College Press.

———, and Karen Hammerness. 2005. "The Design of Teacher Education Programs." In *Preparing Teachers for a Changing World: What Teachers Should Learn and Be Able to Do*, edited by Linda Darling-Hammond and John Bransford, 390–441. San Francisco, CA: Jossey-Bass.

———, Dion Burns, Carol Campbell, A. Lin Goodwin, Karen Hammerness, Ee-Ling Low, and Ken Zeichner. 2017. *Empowered Educators: How High-Performing Systems Shape Teaching Quality around the World*. San Francisco, CA: Jossey-Bass.

———, Ruth Chung Wei, Alethea Andree, Nikole Richardson, and Stelios Orphanos. 2009. *Professional Learning in the Learning Profession: A Status Report on Teacher Development in the United States and Abroad*. Stanford, CA: National Staff Development Council and The School Redesign Network, Stanford University.

Deal, Terrence E., and Allan A. Kennedy. 1982. *Corporate Cultures: The Rites and Rituals of Corporate Life*. Reading, MA: Addison-Wesley.

———. 1983. "Culture and School Performance." *Educational Leadership* 40 (5): 14–15.

Deal, Terrence, E., and Kent D. Peterson. 1999. *Shaping School Culture: The Heart of Leadership*. San Francisco, CA: Jossey-Bass.

De Coster, Isabelle, Bernadette Forsthuber, and Marion Steinberger. 2006. *Quality Assurance in Teacher Education in Europe*. Brussels: Eurydice European Unit.

Dede, Chris. 2010. "Comparing Frameworks for 21st Century Skills." In *21st Century Skills: Rethinking How Students Learn*, edited by James Bellanca and Ron Brandt, 51–76. Bloomington, IN: Solution Tree Press.

Dias-Lacy, Samantha. L., and Ruth V. Guirguis. 2017. "Challenges for New Teachers and Ways of Coping with Them." *Journal of Education and Learning* 6 (3): 265–72.

Elmore, Richard F. 2000. *Building A New Structure for School Leadership*. Washington, DC: Albert Shanker Institute.

Fullan, Michael. 2006. "The Future of Educational Change: System Thinkers in Action." *Journal of Educational Change* 7:113–22.

Fullan, Michael G., and Suzanne Stiegelbauer. 1991. *The New Meaning of Educational Change*. 2nd ed. London: Cassell.
Goodwin, Charles. 2015. "Professional Vision." In *Aufmerksamkeit*, edited by Sabine Reh, Kathrin Berdelmann, and Jorg Dinkelaker, 387-425. Wiesbaden, Germany: Springer VS. https://doi.org/10.1007/978-3-531-19381-6_20.
Good, Thomas L., Bruce J. Biddle, and Ivor F. Goodson. 1997. "The Study of Teaching: Modern and Emerging Conceptions" In *International Handbook of Teachers and Teaching*, edited by Bruce J. Biddle, Thomas L. Good, and Ivor F. Goodson, 67-79. Dordrecht, The Netherlands: Springer.
Hammerness, Karen, Linda Darling-Hammond, John Bransford, David Charles Berliner, Marilyn Cochran-Smith, M. McDonald, and Kenneth M. Zeichner. 2005. "How Teachers Learn and Develop." In *Preparing Teachers for a Changing World: What Teachers Should Learn and Be Able to Do*, edited by Linda Darling-Hammond and John Bransford, 358-89. San Francisco, CA: Jossey-Bass.
Harris, Alma. 2002. *School Improvement: What's in It for Schools?* London: RoutledgeFalmer.
———, and Janet H. Chrispeels, eds. 2006. *Improving Schools and Educational Systems: International Perspectives*. New York: Routledge.
Harris, Alma, and Michelle Jones. 2017. "Leading Professional Learning: Putting Teachers at the Centre." *School Leadership & Management* 37 (4): 331-3. https://doi.org/10.1080/13632434.2017.1343705.
Herbert, Susan, Jennifer Yamin-Ali, and Freddy James. 2018. "Investigating the Nature of Graduates' Classroom Practice: One Step in Transforming the Postgraduate Diploma in Education (Dip. Ed.) Programme." *Caribbean Journal of Education* 40 (1&2): 80-109.
Hirsh, Stephanie. 2009. "A New Definition." *Journal of Staff Development* 30 (4): 10-16.
Hopkins, David. 2001. *School Improvement for Real*. London: RoutledgeFalmer.
Hoyle, Eric. 1986. *The Politics of School Management*. London: Hodder and Stoughton.
Ingersoll, Richard M., Elizabeth Merrill, Daniel Stuckey, and Gregory Collins. 2018. *Seven Trends: The Transformation of the Teaching Force–Updated October 2018*. CPRE Research Reports. Philadelphia, PA: Consortium for Policy Research in Education, University of Pennsylvania Graduate School

of Education. https://repository.upenn.edu /cpre_researchreports/108.

James, Freddy, and Sandra Figaro-Henry. 2017. "Building Collective Leadership Capacity Using Twenty-First Century Digital Tools." *School Leadership and Management* 37 (5): 52–36. https://doi.org/10.1080/13632434.2017.1367277.

Jones, Ken. 2021. "'Professional Development' or 'Professional Learning' ... and Does It Matter?" Education Workforce Council. Accessed 21 May 2021. https://www.ewc.wales/site/index.php/en/about /staff-room/son-archive/43-english/about/staff-room/blog-archive /93-ken-jones-professional-development-or-professional-learning-and-does-it-matter.html.

Kain, Daniel L. 2003. *Problem-Based Learning for Teachers Grades 6-12*. Boston, MA: Pearson Education.

Katz, Steven, Lorna M. Earl, and Sonia Ben Jaafar. 2009. *Building and Connecting Learning Communities: The Power of Networks for School Improvement*. Thousand Oaks, CA: Corwin Press.

Kennedy, Mary M. 1999. "The Role of Preservice Teacher Education." In *Teaching as the Learning Profession: Handbook of Policy and Practice*, edited by Linda Darling-Hammond and Gary Sykes, 54–86. San Francisco, CA: Jossey-Bass.

Lortie, Dan C. 1975. *Schoolteacher: A Sociological Study*. 2nd ed. Chicago: University of Chicago Press.

Louis, Karen Seashore, and Helen M. Marks. 1998. "Does Professional Community Affect the Classroom? Teachers' Work and Student Experiences in Restructuring Schools." *American Journal of Education* 106 (4): 532–75.

McLaughlin, Milbrey Wallin, and Joan E. Talbert. 2006. *Building School-Based Teacher Learning Communities: Professional Strategies to Improve Student Achievement*. New York: Teachers College Press.

Melnyk, Bernadette Mazurek, Ellen Fineout-Overholt, Lynn Gallagher-Ford, and Susan B. Stillwell. 2011. "Evidence-Based Practice: Step by step: Sustaining Evidence-Based Practice through Organizational Policies and an Innovative Model." *The American Journal of Nursing* 111 (9): 57–60.

OECD (Organisation for Economic Co-operation and Development). 2019. *OECD Skills Strategy 2019: Skills to Shape a Better Future*. Paris: OECD Publishing. https://doi.org/10.1787/9789264313835-en.

Opfer, V. Darleen, and David Pedder. 2011. "The Lost Promise of Teacher Professional Development in England." *European Journal of Teacher Education* 34 (1): 3–24.

Pang, Nicholas Sun-Keung, and Ting Wang. 2016. "Professional Learning Communities: Research and Practices across Six Educational Systems in the Asia-Pacific Region." *Asia Pacific Journal of Education* 36 (2): 193–201. https://doi.org/10.1080/02188791.2016.1148848.

Paris, Django. 2012. "Culturally Sustaining Pedagogy: A Needed Change in Stance, Terminology, and Practice." *Educational Researcher* 41 (3): 93–7.

Prosser, Jon. 1999. "The Evolution of School Culture Research." In *School Culture*, edited by Jon Prosser, 1–14. Thousand Oaks, CA: SAGE.

Putnam, Ralph T., and Hilda Borko. 2000. "What Do New Views of Knowledge and Thinking Have to Say About Research on Teacher Learning." *Educational Researcher* 29 (1): 4–15.

Schein, Edgar H. 1992. *Organizational Culture and Leadership*. 2nd ed. San Francisco, CA: Jossey-Bass.

Schleicher, Andreas, ed. 2012. *Preparing Teachers and Developing School Leaders for the 21st Century: Lessons from around the World*. Paris: OECD Publishing. https://doi.org/10.1787/9789264174559-en.

Schoen, La Tefy, and Charles Teddlie. 2008. "A New Model of School Culture: A Response to a Call for Conceptual Clarity." *School Effectiveness and School Improvement* 19 (2): 129–53.

Schwartz, Daniel L., John D. Bransford, and David Sears. 2005. "Efficiency and Innovation in Transfer." In *Transfer of Learning from a Modern Multidisciplinary Perspective*, edited by Jose P. Mestre, 1–51. Greenwich, CT: Information Age Publishing.

Sergiovanni, Thomas J. 1984. "Leadership and Excellence in Schooling." *Educational Leadership* 41 (5): 4–13.

Sheninger, Eric C., and Thomas C. Murray. 2017. *Learning Transformed: 8 Keys to Designing Tomorrow's Schools, Today*. Alexandria, VA: Association of Supervision and Curriculum Development (ASCD).

Southcott, Clare, and Tami McCrone. 2011. *How to Sustain and Replicate Effective Practice*. Berkshire, UK: National Foundation for Educational Research in England and Wales (NFER).

Spiro, Rand J., and Jihn-Chang Jehng. 1990. "Cognitive Flexibility and Hypertext: Theory and Technology for the Nonlinear and Multidimensional Traversal of Complex Subject Matter." In *Cognition, Education, and Multimedia: Exploring Ideas in High Technology*, edited by D. Nix and Rand J. Spiro, 163–205. Mahwah, NJ: Lawrence Erlbaum Associates.

Spiro, Rand J., Paul J. Feltovich, Michael J. Jacobson, and Richard L. Coulson. 1995. "Cognitive Flexibility, Constructivism, and Hypertext: Random Access Instruction for Advanced Knowledge in Ill-Stuctured Domains. *Educational Technology* 31 (5): 24–33.

Stoll, Louise. 1999. "Realising our Potential: Understanding and Developing Capacity for Lasting Improvement." *School Effectiveness and School Improvement* 10 (4): 503–32.

———, and Ray Bolam. 2004. "Developing Leadership for Learning Communities." In *Developing Leadership: Creating the Schools of Tomorrow*, edited by Martin J. Coles and Geoff Southworth, 50–64. New York: Open University Press.

———, and Karen Seashore Louis. 2007. "Professional Learning Communities: Elaborating New Approaches." In *Professional Learning Communities: Divergence, Depth and Dilemmas*, edited by Louise Stoll and Karen Seashore Louis, 1–14. New York: Open University Press.

Thrupp, Martin, and Ruth Lupton. 2010. "Taking School Contexts More Seriously: The Social Justice Challenge." *British Journal of Educational Studies* 54 (3): 308–28.

Timperley, Helen, Aaron Wilson, Heather Barrar, and Irene Fung. 2007. *Teacher Professional Learning and Development: Best Evidence Synthesis Iteration*. Wellington, New Zealand: Ministry of Education.

US NRC (National Research Council). 2000. *How People Learn: Brain, Mind, Experience, and School*. Expanded ed. Edited by John D. Bransford, Ann L. Brown, and Rodney R. Cocking. Washington, D.C.: National Academy Press.

Vescio, Vicki, Dorene Ross, and Alyson Adams. 2008. "A Review of Research on the Impact of Professional Learning Communities on Teaching Practice and Student Learning." *Teaching and Teacher Education* 24 (1): 80–91.

Wenger, Etienne. 1998. *Communities of Practice: Learning, Meaning, and Identity*. Cambridge: Cambridge University Press.

Yamin-Ali, Jennifer. 2014. *Data-Driven Decision-Making in Schools: Lessons from Trinidad*. New York: Palgrave Macmillan.

———. 2021. *Teacher Educator Experiences and Professional Development: Perspectives from the Caribbean*. New York: Palgrave Macmillan.

Zehetmeier, Stefan. 2010. The Sustainability of Professional Development. In *Proceedings of the Sixth Congress of the European Society for Research in Mathematics Education, Lyon, France, January 28–February 1, 2009*, edited by Viviane Durand-Guerrier, Sophie Soury-Lavergne, and Ferdinando Arzarello, 1951–60. Lyon: Institut National de Recherche Pédagogique (INRP).

2. Transfer of Knowledge from the Learning Context to the Practice Context

Introduction

The issue of knowledge transfer from this DipEd programme was examined in a study by Herbert, Yamin-Ali and Ali (2015). That study presented views of the programme provider and its clients and identified areas for negotiation. One of those areas was the knowledge transfer of graduates of the programme. One client representative felt that graduates should not be awarded the diploma until some degree of monitoring had occurred, whereas staff in the programme felt that the programme assessments were reliable and valid; thus graduation signified that "they have achieved a satisfactory level of competence in terms of the programme's objectives" (41). However, one staff member believed that "an energized, excited and willing teacher still needs the practical support of the system of which he or she is a part" (42). The study concluded that the issue of school support required negotiation between the client and provider. This chapter elucidates the nature of graduates' practice. It explores how practitioners in educational administration, foreign languages and science education transferred the knowledge gained in the DipEd learning context to their practice context. Their experiences are presented as cases for each discipline.

> **CASE: EDUCATIONAL ADMINISTRATION**
>
> It must be noted that although all three participants had been trained in educational administration since 2004-9, at the time of the interviews, none had been appointed head of department (HoD), dean, vice-principal or principal. As such, although these participants completed their DipEd in the educational administration specialization, they were functioning as teachers during the time, and their responses reflect the extent to which they were able to transfer their knowledge from both a teacher and a school leader perspective. This observation is valid since the DipEd educational administration specialization combines pedagogy and administration. Subsequent to the interview, the Tobago participant was interviewed for the position and is now appointed HoD. In the interest of anonymity and confidentiality in data reporting, the participants are identified as Alicia, Bernadine and Cassian. They were all employed at denominational schools.

Graduates' Philosophy

Participants' philosophies as school leaders varied. Alicia indicated that her philosophy was that "everyone can learn... and in a school; you don't only have one maximum leader". Alicia noted how her philosophy translates into her practice in that despite not being HoD, she volunteers her expertise to principals, HoDs and the school by training school staff how to conduct clinical supervision and "mentoring novice teachers". Bernadine stated that her philosophy emerged as a result of her involvement in the DipEd programme, and she described her philosophy as viewing education as a "whole system" and feeling "a sense of working more integrated...and more flexible". Cassian's philosophy is that "teachers must strive to become lifelong learners and seek to make the necessary pedagogical changes in order to meet the needs of the twenty-first-century learner". She stated that practising what she preaches was how her philosophy translated into her practice. She also said that for her master's degree thesis, she chose to develop a mentoring programme for novice science teachers.

Reflective Practitioners

All three educators indicated that they were reflective practitioners. Bernadine, however, stated that it was not in a "formal" sense. She explained: "Not in a formal sense, but I do think about what I'm doing, what the students are doing, how they are performing, and I do try to tailor, you know, my practice based on it. But I don't actually, you know, write things down necessarily." Alicia explained that she reflected on her practice and used this reflection to modify her instruction. In her words: "I have to go back to the drawing board and say, 'OK, how can I change my approach to the Form 3?' I can't go with the same approach that I will do with Form 4...so you always have to be reflective." Cassian also used reflection to modify teaching strategies and to influence lesson planning. She explained that she considered herself a reflective practitioner, "because I spend lots of time preparing my lessons to incorporate not just academic content but skills development, including morals and values, I try to self-evaluate by asking students to give feedback on the previous term's teaching strategies".

Instructional Strategies

Participants used different strategies to improve classroom instruction within their department and school. They all spoke to strategies that fostered student-centred approaches. For example, Bernadine focused on her own classroom instruction and used role-playing and technology, such as videos, audio and PowerPoint presentations, as strategies to improve. Additionally, Cassian and Alicia went beyond their classroom practices and sought to develop the instructional capacity of their departments. Cassian focused on the departments in the school. She indicated that she had collaborated with members from other departments to organize a professional learning workshop for teachers on becoming lifelong learners and making changes to meet the needs of the twenty-first-century learner. Alicia focused on what she had done to improve both her instruction and the department's.

Regarding the former, she creates "a class environment that is conducive to learning". She uses questioning as a strategy to guide student thinking and to evaluate whether students have learned. Additionally, at the departmental level, she shares her expertise gained from the DipEd with other department members, mainly through clinical supervision. Cassian also indicated that she had conducted clinical supervision with one novice teacher as part of her master's research work. However, unlike Alicia, she did not routinely engage in this practice at the school. Bernadine did not conduct clinical supervision at all.

Supervision

With regard to the conduct of clinical supervision, both Alicia and Cassian used a robust process involving pre-conference, observation and post-conference, which they attributed to the knowledge and skills that they had gained from participating in the DipEd Educational Administration programme. Despite the fact that none of the participants were HoDs, they all initiated professional learning activities for their teachers, some more extensive than others. In the case of Cassian, she developed one workshop for teachers across the school to grasp the importance of becoming lifelong learners and the need to make the necessary changes to teach students in the twenty-first century. Both Alicia and Bernadine had engaged in professional learning activities, not only within their schools but within the educational division in the case of Alicia and within the Catholic Diocese in the case of Bernadine. Bernadine presented the findings of her DipEd curriculum study, which had focused on the impact of masculine constructs in school, to the school staff and also at a Catholic principals' workshop organized by the Diocese.

Further, she has developed a programme for "ethics" at the school level and trained teachers to use it. Alicia engaged HoDs at the school in professional learning workshops on conducting clinical supervision and preparing students for the School Based Assessment component of their subjects. With regard to the latter, she has conducted workshops at the Education Division for all teachers in Tobago to develop competencies in this area.

Data-driven Decision-making

In terms of whether or not research is used to make decisions in schools, only Alicia said "yes" and explained:

> I am sure it is, and I think it is more now than it was in the past, but, um...I think they can...It's more...? Well, um...I think um...for example, the decision to...to introduce the...the um... the strata, the separation of the gender in Form one. I know that some data was analysed, and so on. I don't know if, you know, it is applied to everything that we do or most of what we do, but um...I think the administration, the principal we have now, is more open to accessing information and ensuring that the...some of the decisions she makes is based on research.

Bernadine and Cassian indicated that they could not say for sure. Only Alicia and Bernadine felt they were somewhat satisfied with the status of teachers' practice at their schools. Alicia felt that 60 per cent of the trained teachers at her school were doing well, while 40 per cent needed improvement. She said:

> Sixty per cent, I would say, of people who are doing well and forty per cent would be where improvements can be made, both in terms of the pedagogy, how the teaching is taking place and also in the person's efficacy, the person's ability to relate and you know...build that...that desire in students to want to learn. Some people don't really care. They go in, and they do their job and....

Bernadine simply indicated that things were better than before and that teachers try. Cassian said no, she was not satisfied with the practice at her school. Nevertheless, it must be noted that neither Bernadine nor Cassian assessed teachers' practice at the school. Alicia, however, indicated that she did assess teachers' practice via the clinical supervision process.

Influence of DipEd on Practice

New knowledge

All participants registered that their involvement in the DipEd programme changed their practice in various ways, although Cassian felt that it was doing the master of education (MEd) degree that inspired her to change. She indicated that although post-DipEd, she was "anxious to implement new ideas" and "was sometimes unable to do so because of a lack of resources" and "many times had to improvise". She described the DipEd as "a stepping stone to the MEd" and explained that she might have been more inspired by the MEd because "the DipEd was crammed into a few months, and I had more time to assimilate the material in the MEd. It was like a light was turned on during that time, and it continues to glow". Ways in which the other participants felt that the DipEd impacted their practice follow.

Culture and Context

Bernadine stated that the DipEd helped her to gain a greater understanding of the context and culture of the school and how these impact teaching and learning, thereby allowing her to adjust her thinking on how to devise instruction that facilitates learning. This she attributed to visiting other schools as part of the DipEd programme. In her words,

> It [DipEd] made me more conscious…in other words, it also made me appreciate what teachers in other schools have to face, so in a sense that when I felt well, OK, this school,

you know, you have demanding students and people who are hard to deal with, it made me more appreciative of what they have to deal with in other schools, and I think that has contributed to my flexibility as well, to know that it's not so bad here. And therefore…it has also made me, I think, and, again, as I say, because we are different, in collaboration with my colleagues, I think some of them still have this idea that at Prestine College, we do things differently, and I have been trying to get them to understand that all of us are teachers, no matter what school you are at, and everybody has challenges to face and people in other schools where they have different kinds of problems and situations are facing up to it and therefore we should.

Networking

Bernadine also felt that her involvement in the DipEd programme helped her recognize the value of networking, and she has made this part of her practice. She went further to say, "It's one of the things that I have…would like to see in this school that we have more networking with teachers from other schools, and so on." As mentioned earlier, Bernadine felt that the DipEd influenced her practice of using technology in her instruction. She commented on the various types of technology she tried using and why she used them, saying:

> …using media. That was a big thing because before, I felt… well again in foreign language, you would use your little CD player and that kind of thing, but using media, accessing videos and doing PowerPoint presentations, that was a big thing because I did not feel confident to do it before. So, I am…that was making things more interactive. I did try to set up a blog with the students, but they're not very responsive to it, but it's still something that I am thinking of. Using blogs and even using, you know, cell phones to do…I do nowadays if I am talking in class about something that's probably a little wider, you know, cultural or historical or so on, and I will tell the students, 'Use the phone. Look it up.' So that is a big thing.

Bernadine further noted that involvement in the DipEd had helped improve her lesson planning.

Leadership

Alicia felt that her exposure to the DipEd programme gave her a better understanding of the leadership role in schools and its impact on school achievement, making her take initiatives to improve the school and view herself as a leader charged with the responsibility to develop teachers and students in the school. In her words, "…when I came back [from doing DipEd], one of the first things I did, my principal then was [name of the principal given], and I went to her, and I said, 'Miss, I am here wherever you need me to do whatever. I'm willing to assist.' Because I realized the…at that point, I realized this task of leading, first of all, it's a lonely one; it's not an easy one, and you cannot do it alone."

She also explained:

> You know, I remember at one point in time, one person was adamant that they get a paper from Education for them to act in a certain position, and they said, 'I'm not going to take up this role until I get the letter from Education', and my position is although today I'm no HoD, I see myself as a HoD. I see myself as a leader in the school, you know, and I believe that if I have certain skills now that I can pass on to other people and I have been around long enough and have had enough, you know, experience under my belt to be able to direct whether it's students or teachers. Why should I wait for a piece of paper to tell me I'm a leader? I'm a leader, and I have made myself; I've gotten enemies from it because some say I am trying to suck up to the principal… because that's our culture. But I did not see it as that. I still don't see it as that…that is why I've taken on added responsibility.

Discussion

There was certainly a culture of "professional orientation" (Schoen and Teddlie 2008) present among all these graduates, evidenced by their initiatives to build capacity within the departments at their schools by providing professional learning activities such as clinical supervision and mentorship. All three graduates expressed a philosophy undergirded by a desire to advance people, even as one advanced oneself, through professional learning. In so doing, they all revealed an intrinsic, albeit embedded, leadership orientation, which motivated them towards human development, and, more specifically, the development of the schools that relate to the "organizational culture" (Schoen and Teddlie 2008). The graduates saw value in learning both individually and collectively and created opportunities and spaces for it to take place in their classrooms, departments and schools, thereby improving the "quality of the learning environment" (Schoen and Teddlie 2008). The graduates used the skills and knowledge gained in the DipEd programme to enlarge the skills and knowledge base within their various school contexts among staff and students. Interestingly, two graduates decided to design mentoring programmes to help novice teachers navigate the teaching and learning spaces within their schools.

Based on these graduates' accounts, the "wider culture" (Prosser 1999) influenced them negatively regarding the Ministry of Education's policy framework for promoting school staff. Therefore, even though they had done a programme of study in educational administration, they remained unpromoted to those positions in their schools, although persons who may not have had educational administration qualifications held those administrative types of position. Similarities like this among all the graduates and others, for example, being in schools where their principals allowed them to use their skills and knowledge from the DipEd to improve teaching and learning in their schools, speak to what Prosser (1999) calls "unique culture".

REFLECTION

It was noteworthy that in delineating their philosophy as school leaders, only Alicia referred to leadership. This might be attributed to the fact that during the interviews, none of the teachers had been designated as HoDs. Consequently, they expressed their educational philosophy from the perspective of educators rather than school administrators. Nevertheless, other data collected from them revealed that they all participate in leadership practices at the school, and they all saw themselves as leaders.

Questions to Discuss – Educational Administration

1. Why would the educational administration participants be considered exemplars in this case?
2. How did the educational administration participants exhibit leadership in this case?
3. What are some common practices that you would want to emulate from the three educational administration cases?

CASE: FOREIGN LANGUAGE

The four foreign language teachers presented in this section comprise one male and three females. At the time of this research, Anthony and Celia taught at seven-year denominational secondary schools, and Brenda and Dana at government secondary schools. They had been teaching at these same schools when they did the DipEd programme.

Graduates' Philosophy

One element common to all four participants was that they saw teaching as going beyond the formal curriculum. Anthony, a teacher at a denominational school, said, "We prepare them for not just the world of work but also to contribute positively to society and make a difference." They all felt that teaching should be student-oriented so that all students' needs are met. This influenced the teaching strategies they employed. Anthony checks what may or may not be working for the students because of their varied learning styles and intelligences, "so we have to be able to cater to all sorts". Brenda, who teaches at a government school, uses repetition, oral work, games and role-play, as well as singing, chanting and clapping the rhythm because her philosophy is that she must reach as many children as she can. Celia's teaching at a denominational school is undergirded by how important she sees the role of values and relationships in her students' lives, so she maintains dialogue with them about these issues. She establishes "student-orientedness" in her teaching by using topics that are relevant to them. Dana, a teacher at a government school, actually prioritizes students' immediate behavioural and social needs over the teaching of the subject: "The problems are multi-layered, so sometimes I find teaching Spanish gets lost in everything else."

Transitioning from the DipEd

The four participants were able to describe how the DipEd had changed them in a general way and how their new perspectives then influenced the strategies they used.

For example, during the DipEd, Dana understood "more about how to structure a class, how to at least try to deliver something". After the programme, she was "a little more confident in the classroom...a little more comfortable with the children...I could handle them, discipline them".

Brenda transitioned into being "an actress, sometimes I have to be a little mad and to go out of the box...I have to say things with a lot of flair when I say it, to excite them...so I'm not who I used to be. I'm different". For Anthony, "there was a transition into a more student-oriented kind of teaching, focusing more on the students and providing opportunities for them to learn and to grow and to appreciate what you think you are doing outside the classroom, seeing the value of what they're learning and...I continue to refine that after DipEd". Celia felt that "teaching in context was a big eye-opener in the DipEd". This feature has definitely been something that she has continued. Collaboration was another feature of the programme she has maintained in her practice. Learning from other teachers in the programme had enabled three of the four to transition from pre-DipEd to during and post-DipEd. For example, Celia indicated she was able to see things that worked and those that did not work, and she got ideas, "things that were out of your comfort zone...like the singing". Her classes would hardly include singing before, but after other teachers in the programme sang with their students, she "tried it and it worked". She also benefited from seeing how other teachers used technology in the classroom and experimented with those ideas in her own setting.

Knowledge Transfer
Student-centredness

What Anthony expressed as the outcome of DipEd for him was, indeed, reflected in his practice in and out of the classroom. The "student-oriented kind of teaching, focusing more on the student", was evident in his proactivity regarding recognizing the need for new teaching and learning materials, which resulted in his development of a teaching text for teachers and students in his department. He explained that it is important to "check what may or may not be working for the students" because he is aware that "students have varied learning styles and intelligences".

There was evidence in all the teachers' lessons and conversations that student-centredness remained with them as a concept that the DipEd programme advocated. In most instances, all four teachers made efforts to plan their lessons in accordance with their students' learning needs and to accommodate effective and meaningful practice. Some lesson plans and delivery showed evidence of the use of revision to link prior knowledge to new, as explained by Anthony, who was "building upon what the students already knew and having them work among themselves and use new vocabulary to expand on prior knowledge". Such ability to diagnose his students' needs is reflected in what he expressed as the outcome of DipEd.

Motivating students might have been a part of their practice prior to the DipEd, as is perhaps evident in Anthony's approach to his students. Apart from teaching materials, the student-centredness extends beyond the physical classroom for him. He felt that "having a good relationship with the students in and out of the classroom would really work for the students and to celebrate their success in a way that is meaningful to them. It doesn't always have to be that I'm giving them a star. For a child, a 'high five' or just a pat on the shoulder might just be the way that they celebrate that they're actually progressing." Brenda was explicitly motivational, using all possible forms of Spanish adjectives to describe the students' oral output.

Student Engagement

Except for one teacher, all demonstrated the ability to engage the students either through lively tone and body language, through questioning and ongoing well-monitored activities, including specially designed ones for weaker students, simulated "Google" activity, giving tips on how to make links and how to remember and use the language, group presentations and the use of competition.

The value of kinesthetics was evident in some lessons. In all the lessons, there was some form of student movement. Students went to the board to write answers; they went to the front of the class to participate in an activity; they used movement to show direction. In Brenda's class, they shrugged in accordance with the stress on a word in Spanish, and word or form drill was accompanied by the use of rhythm through student desk-drumming and foot-stamping. While she used whole-class rote repetition, she also incorporated this practice at the individual level.

Visuals were used by all four teachers in varying ways to enable their students to make connections between language and meaning. Two of the four used technology to portray visual representations of vocabulary items. One used picture charts with words, and another used the whiteboard to draw a family of vocabulary/phrases.

Anthony applied the constructivist approach, which was introduced in the DipEd and explained the value of building upon what the students already knew and having them work among themselves and use new vocabulary to expand on prior knowledge, "as opposed to if I'd probably given them a whole paragraph…and then ask them to write another one". His teaching made numerous explicit attempts to link previous knowledge with the current lesson. For example, he said: "I built it on what they knew. I asked them what they knew about Carnival, the vocabulary, I'd see what they could have transferred there…and they sat among themselves and worked out the material. I didn't give them anything to say what… how the paragraph should be. So they created the work, and I'm thinking that, for me, that's a student-oriented classroom." Another technique that built on students' prior knowledge was the presentation of a graphic organizer to begin a lesson, after which the students used a bubble to enter language they already knew. He said, "Each child is finding his or her own way to process…and assimilate information." He also enabled his students to see links between elements of the lesson. For example, he highlighted the link between discrete phrases introduced and the overall theme of the lesson. From time to time, he told the students what they would be doing next in the lesson and also shared with them what they would be doing in the following lesson.

Celia advised the students to look for links to help with meaning when reading in the target language. She also predicted what help the students would need and prepared a simulated Google tutorial on verbs to support their learning during the lesson. She created a mnemonic designed to help the students remember the French subject pronouns and aided their conceptual understanding by using the metaphor of a sandwich to help students structure the negative form of the verb in French (*ne* verb *pas*). The student-centred approach enabled all four teachers to use pair work for oral practice. Anthony used group work for a collaborative activity where students help each other to write. In his classes, interactivity was visible in the standard set-up of the classrooms for forms 3 and 4, which were organized for group work. This facilitated his frequent use of role-play and group work. Three of the four teachers used closure in their lessons, helping students to consolidate their learning before leaving the classroom.

Ability to Plan Lessons

The four teachers used lesson plans and designed resources required to deliver the lessons. Their plans for the lessons observed for this research included topic, objectives, previous knowledge, set induction, activities, evaluation and closure. However, the lesson objectives varied in strength. While most of them were functional, meaning that they used linguistic functions like "ask for", "describe" and "inquire about", others, as in the case of Brenda, were vague or did not consist of linguistic functions, for example, "review", "read", "say". In the case of Celia, there was one vague objective "to talk about…." Generally, there was some evidence in the plans of using revision to link prior knowledge to new concepts, and overall, plans indicated attention to a variety of linguistic skills, demonstrating the possibility of integration and interdependence of skills.

Lesson phases generally flowed and were well-timed for suitable pace, except for one instance when there was insufficient time allocated for teaching and practice before the evaluation phase. Dana's practice showed evidence of a well-structured lesson plan. Evaluation aligned with the lesson's objectives in each case. Interestingly, this is one of the outcomes she had hoped to gain from the programme: "I realized I needed to learn how to actually structure a class. I didn't know how to really plan a class. So that has certainly helped me now in how to structure a class. The DipEd, I think…made me understand more about how to structure a class, how to at least try to deliver something."

Although not the official head of the department, Brenda plans the scheme of work for the other Spanish teachers from Forms 1 to 5: "I plan it for everybody… from Form 1 to Form 5 and they use it. I put guidelines, I put scenarios you can use…." She evidently had gained the confidence to do this.

Planning lessons has been the norm at Celia's school where they use shared schemes of work monitored by the head of department, who is a DipEd graduate and shares the core principles of foreign language teaching as taught in the programme so that she expects lessons to reflect those. She sums it up by saying, "I can safely say that DipEd has helped, has really helped this department."

Anthony explained, "On the DipEd programme, apart from how you structure your lesson, the activities you use within the lesson and then how you evaluate, those have stayed with me throughout from what I've learnt in the programme."

All four teachers' strong student-centredness enabled them to be flexible and creative within the generic lesson plan structure they had learned in the programme. The types of activities documented on the lesson plans reflected this responsiveness to student needs.

Communicative Approach and the Use of Context

The main principle underlying foreign language pedagogy, as advocated in the DipEd programme is the communicative approach. Generally, all teachers spoke mostly in English throughout the foreign language class, with intermittent instructions or statements in the target language (TL). They all greeted the students in the TL at the beginning of each lesson. They all used the students' names to address them, and they used context to drive their lessons, but to varying degrees. There were some instances of the grammar-translation approach. Still all four teachers expressed an affinity with the use of context as an enabler in foreign language learning, and in most instances, lesson plans included contexts. For example, Celia said, "I definitely think the context, teaching in context, was a big eye-opener in the DipEd, and so that has definitely been something I continued." This was exemplified in one of her lessons where the use of "can" and "have to" was framed within the context of living in Guadeloupe and working part-time to earn money. She consistently re-introduced the context of the lesson to keep them engaged and to make their learning meaningful.

Anthony "leans towards interactive instruction", which was observed in the physical set-up of his classroom for group work. He further explains that "Spanish is not a content-based subject, so you want the students to develop the skills that they will have to use in the language, see the language used in a real context, or say things that they will actually have to say in real contexts, in real life." He used linguistic functions and situations or scenarios throughout his lessons to make the content and practice as authentic as possible.

Brenda described her planning like this: "I think about real life. When would they have a chance to use this? In real life. How? In what area? And then I try to devise or maybe bring that area in the classroom…Even if it is like a situation and we are doing written work, it's a situational scenario that I give them." Brenda appears to be a convinced user of context in her teaching.

In the case of Dana, very little target language was used, and at times, she requested translation from Spanish to English instead of using an inductive approach to facilitate comprehension. Linguistic functions were underutilized. For example, the teacher said to a student: "Ask (student's name) *qué haces los fines de semana*?" instead of saying "find out from (a student) what he or she does on weekends.'"

Generally, lesson segments showed where activities were designed to practise the language required for the context presented. However, while contexts were purposefully introduced in some segments of the lessons of all four teachers, they were not always sustained throughout the lessons in some instances. Three of the four teachers recognized the value of role-play in communicative language teaching and infused this type of activity into their lessons.

Classroom Ethos

Although lesson planning and choice of activities generally reflected student-centredness, the discipline and classroom management approach tended to lean towards teacher-centredness, with the teacher taking control. The teacher's presence was strong in each case, especially with Dana, who continually admonished students for errant behaviour such as late-coming, incorrect uniform, non-attentive behaviour and untidy classroom. At least she was aware of the students' participation or lack thereof, as she said, "Toni, you are dreaming this afternoon. Wake up." She commented on the school context, specifically the students' background, as being a challenge to her teaching and, consequently, classroom management: "Children with literacy challenges", "learning disabilities", "from very disadvantaged homes". "School is just a place to be during the day." "More than half the intake is remedial." "Behaviour is always a problem." In light of these challenges in her school,

Dana felt that "the DipEd programme is more for an average to ideal situation". She did not feel that it adequately prepared her for teaching in her context. In this case, the teacher's actions reflected a lack of skills to handle classroom management issues in her context.

All four teachers tried to spread their questions to a variety of students, but Brenda sometimes asked only volunteers, eliminating responses from the non-volunteers. Anthony was unaware of one group's non-collaboration, and Brenda could not capture incorrect practice during a whole group drill.

Attention to Students' Non-academic Needs

In all four cases, however, the classroom ethos and the teachers' comments reflected not only the will to help students learn the subject content but also a desire to build their self-esteem. Dana, who reported many challenges in her school context, revealed the following about her students:

> They know I care about them. They would still come and talk to me and greet me on the corridor...even some of the really tough boys...they would come and greet me and take my bag and say, "Hi Miss" and that kind of thing, so in how I relate to them, I'm still kind to them, even though some of them are quite difficult...so I've learnt how to do that because I understand they all have a story, they all have a very difficult story behind them. So, I'm kind to them and respectful, very respectful of them. Even the most miserable ones.

Brenda, teaching at a government school, had indicated that her persona had been transformed into that of an actress to keep her students engaged. That willingness to behave "outside the box" extended to outside the classroom when she became aware that the students wanted an "upscale" graduation. She exerted much effort, even after her colleagues felt an upscale hotel was beyond the students' reach. "The Hyatt? You want to carry them there?" Brenda said, "...and a lot of teachers laughed." But with the support of her colleagues at the school, funds were raised to subsidize the students' graduation at their desired venue. In light of this, Brenda said, "I categorize myself as a pioneer."

Celia's classes reflect a student-oriented ethos. She commented:

> So, I think relationships are definitely important, between the students and the teachers, creating relationships among students and traditional things like respect...things like just being able to be polite and sharing/caring...especially with our boys. I have a real passion for working with boys...I tend to ask my students a lot about how they feel. I try to be in touch with them. So, I try to use stuff that I know would impact them...and I also try to feel them out like they come into the classroom and something has happened, and I will try to have a discussion with them. If I find they're not getting along, I'll usually ask them to tell me what the problem is.

Anthony, along with his colleagues, realized the following:

> There was a problem with the boys, and there was a Boys' Day; and instead of just carrying a programme and giving the boys a lecture or anything, I took it upon myself to go to the upper school boys and do a survey "What would you like to see happen if it's a Boys' Day...They got to talk about what they wanted to talk about, and then there were fun activities, interactive activities with their teacher, so therefore they saw us then in a different light.

Technology Integration

Brenda was one of the four teachers who used technology effectively to facilitate learning through the use of the multimedia projector. She used a video of French students discussing the lesson's topic and presented graphics with accompanying vocabulary. She also successfully simulated the use of "Google" without using the internet. Brenda also used the projector in place of handouts and was efficiently able to borrow another projector to use in her lesson when her projector bulb blew. Her school actively promotes the use of technology in teaching, and there is a sharing of resources and ideas in the department. In addition to using technology to present images and videos to support vocabulary acquisition and as stimuli for practice activities, she uses technology to facilitate students' oral assessments, where students upload their orals using software. In addition, they "post the questions or the reading passage and [the students] tape it". "An electrical problem" in the school prevents Brenda from using technology. She "doesn't bother to use the tape recorder" because she's "gotten frustrated with it over the years".

Anthony uses technology along with the rest of the department. "We actually create audio material through "Text Aloud.'" However, he says, "I would love to use technology more often in my classes, but given the challenges we have here, I've reached the point where I want to shy away from using [it]." He says that the technology equipment they have at the school is usually "malfunctioning".

Dana presented still graphics in her lessons, accompanied by vocabulary. She related that there was only one multimedia projector in the school, and there was a lot of competition for using the room where it is permanently located. So she uses pictures and other visuals, which she sticks on a blackboard.

Learning from DipEd Research

For Brenda, the action research that she conducted in the DipEd programme has helped her in her current teaching. She says: "My DipEd research, the curriculum research, was moving from oral work into written work, and I still use it today to get them to write. I do a lot of oral practice and role-play, so once they can say it, they can act it out; they could bring it back to me. It's easy for them when it comes to writing. So, I still use it. I still do the peer correction, and I still do the brain-storming."

Anthony was sufficiently motivated to continue to do research at the master's level: "I'm doing a research with my fourth form class. The problem I was observing was writing skills, poor writing skills and demotivation." Informal research into students' needs has resulted in the creation of a booklet for students' use in foreign language learning from first to fifth form levels.

For Celia, articles of interest are shared among the department to guide their teaching: "You would have an article that would tell you something. You would try it out... reading and sharing." Dana does not conduct formal research. She didn't seem to feel that the formal research that she had conducted in the DipEd would likely recur in her regular teaching practice.

Generally, the four teachers do not conduct formal research into their teaching except for a requirement, as in the case of Anthony. However, they reflect on their teaching, as is seen below.

Reflective Practitioner

Brenda clearly reflects on her teaching. She explains as follows: "Sometimes I sit down, I think of what could I have done better...to improve this. Well, some days you'll find that you cannot reach the students...so I would sit down and say, 'What else I could have done?' You know? Or, they just seem a little...lacklustre...I would...say, 'Well...maybe something happen (*sic*) with them, maybe that triggered them off...'" She shares these thoughts with her colleagues: "We are always talking about classes and what to do and any problems we encounter." Dana's reflection guides her teaching. She stated, "On a personal basis, I may try something, and if it doesn't work out, try it with another class, maybe because sometimes one thing works with a class and one doesn't for the other class."

Anthony reflects, "a lot...because I need to know where I'm at, how what I'm doing is impacting on the students...what can I do differently because even though the booklets are there, each year we teach the strategies differently...The material is there, but we implement it in a different way to see how we can bring about...different results in the students. So I'm always trying to find a way to refine what I do so that the students can benefit." Similarly, Celia says, "I tend to do a lot of reflection on how did my class go. Part of our lesson plan usually includes a little part to comment on how we felt the lesson went. Sometimes I write it down, sometimes I just [think about it] ... and I tend to ask for feedback from my students, and then I would look at what they have said."

Discussion

In the foreign language teachers' practice, transfer of learning contributed to school culture in terms of teachers' professional orientation, the quality of the learning environment, and a student-centred focus on teaching and learning. These three dimensions, identified by Schoen and Teddlie (2008) as three components of school culture, were seen to be interconnected within the lessons observed. The teachers' professional orientation was apparent in their activities and attitudes, such as willingness to collaborate (for three of the teachers) and keeping their students' learning at the forefront of their planning. The quality of the learning environment was influenced by their approach to teaching, which they had transferred from the DipEd programme, whether it was 'becoming an actress' or simply teaching in context or using technology to enhance delivery. There was also cohesion between their actions and their espoused teaching philosophy. They were now influencing their context and school culture having introduced new or enhanced professional behaviours in and out of the classroom. The one teacher's diminished capacity to transfer much learning is seen to be linked to the "wider culture" (Prosser 1999), which saw the infiltration of wider social factors, possibly linked to socio-economic factors, as debilitating.

REFLECTION

These teachers articulated their philosophy of teaching as one that was clearly humanistic. In addition, they were also pragmatic when it came to developing their students' life skills. The common approach is significant since they come from schools different from each other's. While all teachers demonstrated the capacity to be reflective, each school context appeared to influence the teacher's active response to their reflection, demonstrating transfer of learning from the programme to their teaching context. However, while a teacher might have reflected on her practice, the programme might not have equipped her to act upon what she perceived to be her students' challenges.

Questions to Discuss – Foreign Language

1. Which aspects of knowledge transfer from the programme do you find useful in teaching a foreign language?
2. What are some commonalities in these teachers' approaches to teaching?
3. How are these teachers similar to or different from you in how they practise in the classroom?

CASE: SCIENCE TEACHING

This section introduces the four graduates of the science specialization who participated in the research. Wilhelminah and Mahalia were employed at seven-year denominational (government-assisted) schools in Trinidad. Sophia and Peter were employed at five- and seven-year government schools in Trinidad and Tobago, respectively.

Graduates' Philosophy

All teachers endorsed the belief, as articulated in national educational documents, that all children can learn and indicated that they adopted a student-centred approach to teaching/learning to address students' needs. For example, according to Wilhelminah:

> Well over the years what I have seen as a teacher and from experience I see that we would teach with a general method, the textbook method, you put the examples on the board, the general traditional method. But what I saw for some children, you had to slow it down, do more concrete examples and try to bring the class in such a way that you could reach the slower children as well.

The teachers strongly believe that students must be involved in the learning process, as Sophia indicates:

> Sometimes, I think for me it's about me stopping and saying to myself, it's not about me giving the knowledge all the time, that research also says that students are also capable of acquiring that knowledge and it's for me to set up scenarios for them to acquire that knowledge. I think that specifically for science though, it actually gives…it lends itself to actually getting them to do things and to acquire that knowledge for themselves.

Mahalia believed that learning is facilitated when students discern the relevance of the concepts/ideas to everyday life (or to other disciplinary concepts) and that learning is about understanding and not simply regurgitation:

> So, my philosophy is what you learn it must have some relationship so you could see it applied if even not to your life personally. It must be applied in the real world. Some would say yes, imagination. I would say pragmatic. I would say so. Your ideals. I don't believe in compromising your ideals per se, but even if you could understand where you coming from, well, to me, that is a start. So, I would say the way in which I learn is through understanding and not through cramming.

Similar to Mahalia, Peter believes that students must be engaged in the learning process and that deep learning is facilitated when students discern relationships among concepts. He explains: "…what I would have them do is try to build a concept for each section in groups and combine them to have them understand that once you build a visual picture, you get a deeper learning than just having a series of words where you can't see the picture or the relation."

Overall, the teachers believe that learning is facilitated by having students take responsibility for preparing before class, participating and being engaged during class and spending time on their studies after class.

In expressing their student-centredness philosophy, all teachers expressed high expectations for their students. They believed that they could succeed, but they also believe that students must be actively engaged in and committed to the learning process. For example, Wilhelminah has high expectations of students but believes they need to spend more time on their studies. She says, "…and they don't go home and study enough." However, she encourages student responsibility and ownership of learning through student research, class presentations and problem-solving. For example, at the upper levels, she uses the Jigsaw approach, and students are expected to research topics and use presentation software to present information to their peers. Sophia also has high expectations of students and encourages student participation in the teaching-learning process. "I think that specifically for science, though… it lends itself to actually getting them to do things and to acquire that knowledge for themselves. Sometimes, I get them to do the research themselves, do presentations, sometimes it may be problems, ask them, give them a scenario a little problem and ask them to solve."

Teachers also exhibited high self-efficacy and deliberately used strategies intended to effect learning and interest. Wilhelmina indicated: "A lot of times you may have one of them being able to say 'Well, Miss, I know,' even if it's not the entire class. So, we have a SMART board. I actually used it once this term...and I realized that they, again, the students seemed very much interested." However, students' response to new strategies is sometimes negative, causing Sophia to question whether a student-centredness philosophy is appropriate in her context. She lamented:

> To me students always take the easy route. I have never come across in my entire teaching tenure here doing that activity in Form 1. I actually have to force them if it is to do a play or do something else. I don't know if they are not seeing it. Perhaps if they saw it in action, they could replicate, but they are probably so accustomed to doing things one way, they continue.

Like Wilhelminah, Mahalia's philosophy of student involvement in the learning processes was espoused, and she had high expectations that students would engage in reading and relevant research prior to class sessions, which would then be designed as a discussion-type format (a flipped classroom format). Her high expectations were not always met, and, accordingly, there was concern and monitoring of students "who are at risk if they are not attaining a certain level". In these circumstances, parents' input was requested, and efforts were made to assist. Peter also expressed high expectations that students should have an input in the learning process by asking questions and by constructing their knowledge through the development of concept maps. But like Sophia, he recognized the role of habits and past experiences of teacher/student interaction. He indicated that to have students adopt this new active role is "an uphill battle, as we are all creatures of habit, so the students are more leaning to just answering questions".

Knowledge Transfer

Transfer of knowledge from the learning context to the practice context is premised on the concept of sustainability, which is linked to the impact of the programme. The analysis of interview data revealed that science graduates' views about the impact of the programme on their practice ranged from the assimilation of ideas into their traditional practice to the transformation of practice resulting from a paradigm shift toward a more student-centred focus. For example, Peter stated, "The fact that I am shifting and making it more student-centred, that came straight out of DipEd." Mahalia felt strongly that the DipEd impacted teachers' practice. She felt any lack of evidence of the impact of the DipEd on teachers' practice was not related to programme features. She opined that the qualities and characteristics of the individual teacher were more likely the reason for inaction. Alluding to the idea that, at a minimum, some of the ideas to which they were exposed in the programme could be assimilated into their practice, she said: "But you have to be a real slacker or indifferent person not to use at least one thing that you learnt on DipEd. I have spoken to some teachers, even if [it] is one thing they use, [it] is the set induction."

Aligned with their espoused views, the science teachers' actions in the practice context and the nature of their practice provided evidence of the impact and influence of the knowledge gained and ideas to which they were exposed in the learning context.

Lesson Planning

The selected science teachers were generally well-prepared for the lessons observed, as evidenced by the availability of lesson plans and resources required. Three of the four teachers prepared complete lesson plans using the lesson template which was introduced in the DipEd programme. Consequently, the lesson plans presented comprised concept statements, objectives, set induction, activities for lesson development and consolidation. The fourth teacher prepared lesson notes. For the complete written lesson plans presented, the concept statements were fairly well written, with varying levels of adherence to criteria advanced during the training in the DipEd programme. That is, the concept statements comprised elements of lesson content, context and relevance of the big science idea, but not all elements were consistently presented. For example, for a lesson on the topic "Writing chemical formulae with polyatomic ions" within a unit on chemical bonding, the concept statement was presented as follows: "A polyatomic ion is a group of atoms with a specific charge and must be treated as a single entity when used in a chemical formula. The size of the charges of a polyatomic cation or anion must balance with their respective counterparts in a chemical formula." It was noted that a statement on relevance was not included. The quality of the written objectives varied. In some instances, the objectives were not written in full conformity with the recommended format, for example, the use of a single action verb, or were not classified at varying levels of Bloom's taxonomy, or they focused on lower-level thinking outcomes. A variety of resources, including worksheets and guides for practical activity, were available; and the teachers also planned deliberately to link students' prior knowledge to the concepts to be introduced. For example, one science teacher included the following review questions on the written plan for a lesson on the structure and function of the heart: "How many chambers make up the heart? Why are valves necessary? What is the name of the main artery?" The teachers also planned for formative and summative assessments.

Teachers espoused the value of lesson planning and provided lesson plans. However, their comments revealed that there can be resistance to the idea of preparing formal written plans. Wilhelminah referred to the relationship between planning and teacher effectiveness while also commenting on teachers' responses in general to planning: "We learnt about lesson planning when we came to DipEd. Thank God. But the lesson planning and the practice of doing it, the clinical supervision, I think it makes you a better teacher. Yes, the teachers quarrel about it...It keeps you on your toes. And you actually sit down and think how you're going from Stage A to Stage B in a lesson." Mahalia espoused similar views of the value of planning but also expressed her personal experience of planning after DipEd as a hindrance:

> What the DipEd helped me with was planning, making the lesson interesting, different methods of teaching. Like the Jigsaw...So that is what I liked about DipEd. It showed you about the lesson plan and the set induction...I understand the value of the format of the lesson plan. But actually, for me now, in practice, it hinders me. ...So DipEd for me...The majority of what they teach you in Dip Ed, I won't say that it don't (sic) apply. It's probably just me personally. The only thing that I really used from DipEd was the Bloom's taxonomy. That helped me a lot with planning the lesson and probably the time management aspect.

Classroom Management

Teachers felt that the ideas presented during the DipEd with respect to grouping students and management of student behaviour were relevant to their practice. Consequently, teachers transferred and sustained these strategies to their practice. For example, Sophia referred to her use of group work and student discipline as outcomes of exposure to DipEd: "So, what I would say, that is one thing I learned from the DipEd. So, it kind of structured how I gave students their group work. So, it's not like some teachers, when I talk to them...Sometimes too I do this especially a lot with the Form ones, put them in groups...Classroom management, you know, the discipline, it would have helped with that."

Classroom management outcomes were evident during the classroom observations. All four teachers adopted the whole class model for delivery, with group work organized for practical activities. During these sessions, very good classroom management was demonstrated by all four teachers, with students on task and meaningfully engaged throughout the lesson and with teachers monitoring and evaluating student progress. There was little need or no need for reminders about the rules of engagement and classroom policies and procedures, which were well established. There were good interpersonal relations between teachers and students. There was also good time management, and the lessons were completed as planned, with closure and consolidation of learning within the allotted time.

The Reflective Habit

The DipEd programme aims to develop the reflective practitioner, and opportunities are provided for reflection on practice as part of the practicum course, as well as through students' exposure to action research. Wilhelminah mentioned her natural disposition towards reflection. "But I think I normally would reflect on it and...so I think it was even reinforced when I did the DipEd." Sophia provided an insight into her reflection-in-action and reflection-on-action:

> It has influenced me a lot – having us reflect. Actually, even with that practice of having us reflect, you know, what it is we are actually doing in the classroom. I tend to do a lot of that. Sometimes it may be I think of other ways, maybe I did a lesson today; and I don't think it was well received by the children. Sometimes, I probably...like the introduction. I don't think it was good enough. What else could I have done to actually start that lesson? So that in terms of reflecting, yes, a lot of that is done.

All teachers mentioned the value of reflection, but there were also indicators from Mahalia that systems within the practice context, such as the use of record and forecast books, do not support or encourage reflection. Mahalia said:

> Whereas when I write it long hand, I am seeing it and if even I write it out neatly. So, it helps in a sense with reflection... We have a record and forecast book, but I use that to say what lesson I am going to do today. To keep track. And even the record and forecast book, I will say to you it doesn't facilitate reflection. It has class, lesson, date.

Significantly, none of the teachers provided examples of written reflections on their lessons since they graduated from the programme. It appears that this aspect of reflection was not transferred.

Instructional Strategies

Most of the four science teachers mentioned a paradigm shift from teacher-centred to student-centred instruction. Classroom observations revealed a mix of strategies catering to the needs of learners, as well as to the nature of science, including practical activities, the use of analogies and models, questioning, and the use of ICT.

Practical Activities

Practical work is integral to science teaching, and while enrolled in the DipEd programme, teachers are encouraged to use practical activities to enhance conceptual understanding. All of the selected science teachers facilitated practical work in at least one of the lessons observed. These sessions were mainly held in the science laboratory setting. In the case of Mahalia, the equipment and apparatus were brought to the Form 1 classroom for practical work to provide hands-on experience with the apparatus and to develop skills in measurement. However, the session was conceptualized as a demonstration with a few students involved in the actual use of equipment. In most instances observed, the practical work was intended to facilitate concept development in what one teacher referred to as a "teaching lab". The sessions observed were in the main illustrative of "guided inquiry". For example, the teacher stated, "I want you to follow the instructions, and then we will discuss your observations." In one case, students were developing concepts related to electrolysis; in another, the Form 4 students were introduced to the activity series and were provided with opportunities for inductive reasoning, and in the third, concepts related to the structure and function of the eye were addressed. In those instances, groups of students were assigned to apparatus and materials along with a worksheet as a guide. For one session observed, the lab was a requirement for the School Based Assessment (SBA). It was used to assess students' competencies in using science process skills, such as measurement, observation and data analysis. In planning the SBA session, there was insufficient apparatus and materials for each student, so again, students were assigned to groups to share materials and equipment. At the same time, each student gained hands-on experience with each component of the investigation. During practical work, students were required to make observations, collect and analyse data. For example, the session on rates of reaction required students to measure time versus concentration, convert time to rate, plot graphs of the data, recognize the pattern of change and propose a generalization through a process of inductive reasoning. Having established principles by engaging in practical activity, students were also required to apply the generalization to specific new situations by engaging in deductive reasoning. But high levels of intellectual engagement were not restricted to practical activities, as theory sessions, mainly with Form 6 students, also required recognition of patterns, for example.

Use of Analogies and Models

Analogies and models are promoted within the DipEd programme as strategies to aid science learning. They are intended to help students understand abstract concepts based on familiar concrete examples located within their everyday experiences. The selected science teachers used a variety of analogies based on students' experiences. In most instances, the teachers provided a predetermined analogy. In teaching a Form 3 class about bonding, Wilhelminah compared the bonding between atoms to the bond of human relationships. During Sophia's lesson on the circulatory system in a Form 4 Integrated Science class, the analogies employed were the pump and the hose; in Peter's lesson about homeostasis, he presented the analogy of the tap and switch to students and in teaching about the structure and function of the eye, used comparisons to the camera, projector and screen to illustrate his point. In one instance, students' input was required to develop an analogy for the rate determining step. In teaching a Form 6 class about reaction mechanisms and the rate determining step, Mahalia used students' prior experiences to provide a concrete example but also required their input in developing an analogy for the rate determining step as follows:

> T: Let's go back to when we get up in the morning. One, think about your ritual – the steps you have to work with to get ready to reach here (school). What takes you the longest time to do?"
>
> S: Travelling
>
> S: Ironing my shirt
>
> T: So, I remember my sister, when she starts to get ready. She finishing everything but like a whole half an hour in front of the mirror with that hair. And we can't leave until that hair… So you all get that, right? So you may have many steps to follow or to go through, but that one stage will determine how long it is going to take, and that is what we call the rate determining step. The slow step.

Wilhelminah also referred to her use of models in teaching science. "We had them actually build models of the cell."

Questioning

Science teachers were exposed to sessions on questioning as a key strategy for concept development in science. Particularly in relation to inquiry and discovery learning, issues related to teachers' questioning techniques and the role of wait time were included in the DipEd science curriculum. The classification of questions in accordance with Bloom's taxonomy, the importance of students' questions and principles of test development were also introduced. The science graduates referred to these sessions on questioning and the learning outcomes. In so doing, they revealed that the theories and principles introduced in the DipEd programme were still being considered within their practice context. Mahalia said: "At least now I know. We had a thing with questioning, how to question, how to make up your paper, how to increase in intensity. I mean, I could tell you before some of it is intuitive, eh? You know, okay, don't give them a hard question to start." Wilhelminah also referred to the concept of wait time, stating that "I guess we should give students time to answer a question. You know how we usually jump in." Sophia and Peter endorsed Wilhelminah's view. Sophia stated that "with the questioning, if you want to be effective, you must have sufficient wait time". Graduates' reflection on their use of questioning strategies also revealed concerns about their proficiency within the practice context when compared with best practices introduced in the DipEd programme. For example, Mahalia recognized shortcomings with respect to her questioning technique and the challenges experienced in conceptualizing and managing responses to open-ended questions. She commented as follows:

> With the questioning and then too even with me, sometimes I still think I have to work on the questioning in the sense... um, I don't want you asking me questions if my questions are not doing it properly. It could confuse them. So, personally, I think I have to work on the questioning so that I don't confuse them, especially when you're dealing with topics that have all these different links. So, in that sense, I tend to ask more closed questions. I still haven't really perfected the open-ended questions. And even with the open questions, I tend not to because then I'll lead into discussion and then question, question, and like how my mind works too, when I'm on a topic, it's hard for me to disengage now to go back to a next topic.

Classroom observations revealed that science graduates asked a range of questions during whole class sessions, from those requiring recall to those pitched at the level of synthesis in accordance with Bloom's taxonomy. However, they tended to ask a higher proportion of questions at the level of application and above when teaching the higher forms (4-6) than they did when teaching Forms 1-3. In all of the classrooms observed, students asked fewer questions than their teachers did. It was noted, however, that Form 6 science students tended to ask more questions than students in lower-school science classrooms. In keeping with principles of student involvement in the learning process introduced in the DipEd, Wilhelminah organized student presentations at the upper-secondary level and facilitated student questioning. In this Form 6 class, students were responsible for explaining reactions in organic chemistry to and for asking questions of their peers. Similarly, during Mahalia's session on reaction mechanisms in the topic "Rates of Reaction" at the Form 6 level, student questions were encouraged. The number of students' questions was approximately equal to the number of teacher's questions.

Technology Integration: Use of ICT

With the prevalence of digital technology within today's society, teachers in the DipEd programme are exposed to a module on technology integration for learning with a focus on ICT. Two of the four science teachers used ICT during the lessons observed. In one case, a video was used as the set induction for the Form 4 session on electrolysis; in another, the Lower 6 students were required to present their research on an aspect of organic chemistry to the rest of the class, and this session was held in the multimedia room with internet access. The students prepared a PowerPoint with embedded videos. For this latter teacher as well, delivery of the Form 3 class was supported with PowerPoint slides. Teachers' use of ICT extended beyond the use of gadgets while in direct face-to-face contact with students, as they also reminded students that notes and other resources were or would be emailed. In one instance, Peter, who did not use ICT during the session that was observed, requested that students use the internet for further research.

Discussion

The dimensions of school culture which were most applicable to the analysis of data from the classroom observations were "quality of the learning environment" and "student-centred focus" (Schoen and Teddlie 2008). An analysis of data from lessons observed in terms of the quality of the learning environment, where the quality of the learning environment is interpreted to mean the level of intellectual engagement, the availability of resources for teaching and learning and the level of student participation (Schoen and Teddlie 2008, 141) reveal that the science learning environments were mainly teacher-directed and controlled. For example, there were teacher-developed analogies to aid concept development and teacher-designed practical activities with students following the teachers' directives and instructions. The tasks and activities provided some opportunities for higher-order thinking, although in most instances, especially at the lower-secondary levels, students were asked primarily to recall and demonstrate understanding. The upper-school students were provided more opportunities for autonomy and to demonstrate leadership and higher-order thinking than the younger students. Teacher oral questioning was meant to stimulate intellectual engagement; however, some teachers have not yet perfected their questioning techniques. Questioning continues to be a work in progress. Practical work at the upper-secondary levels facilitated high levels of intellectual engagement. However, instances of problem identification, opportunities to plan and design experiments and to engage in evaluative thinking and decision-making, also reflective of high levels of student intellectual engagement, were not observed. Resources for laboratory work and ICT integration were available upon request and contributed to a high-quality learning environment.

The analysis revealed that lessons were routinely delivered to the class as a whole, with no intentional plans for differentiation according to student ability or student interest. Planned group work was not based on student differences but as a strategy for peer interaction and sharing of equipment and materials and mainly to provide hands-on experiences. The actions which participants displayed stand in contrast to the student-centred focus dimension espoused by Schoen and Teddlie (2008, 141), which "is concerned with assessing the extent to which the needs of individual students are met by the school's programs, policies, rituals, routines and traditions". However, teachers did stop the lesson to address issues related to individual misunderstandings or lack of clarity, either when students signalled the need for assistance or when they observed students' facial expressions or body language. Teachers also gave individualized attention to students formally diagnosed with a learning disability. Thus, there was a high quality of planning and implementation competence in terms of teacher-selected activities but low quality in terms of student autonomy and control. The science sessions observed were situated more toward the teacher-directed end of a continuum that ranges from teacher direction and control to student autonomy and control.

REFLECTION

The science teachers all articulated a philosophy of student-centredness in the learning interaction, as well as care and concern for students' progress. However, they perceived that many students were reluctant to participate in active learning strategies which underpin student-centred approaches to science learning. Teacher direction and control is clearly the default position for the four science graduates, with highly structured planning, teachers' selection of learning outcomes and strategies for delivery and concept development through questioning. However, opportunities for group work, some student responsibility for learning and for higher-order thinking, especially at the upper-secondary level are provided, although within tightly defined content boundaries. It is significant that science students were not observed in activities which require them to plan and design experiments or to experience problem-based learning which contextualizes science and develops higher-order thinking skills. While seemingly paradoxical, it is evident that within the practice context, the teachers developed a philosophy of student-centredness which accommodates many of the strategies for student-centredness introduced in the DipEd, although their practice is dominated by traditional arrangements for teaching.

Questions to Discuss – Science

1. What are the implications if students do not have opportunities to develop higher-order thinking within the classroom?

2. What are your experiences in using practical work and analogies in science teaching?

3. How can teachers resolve the issue of students' resistance to student-centred approaches?

Conclusion

This chapter examined the nature of graduates' practice. It explored how practitioners in the disciplines of educational administration, foreign languages and science education transferred the knowledge gained in the DipEd learning context to their practice context. A synthesis across the cases reveals that graduates have transferred some of what they learned in the DipEd into their practice context. The ways in which the DipEd influenced graduates' practice can be categorized as encouraging them to:

1. Take initiative in their schools
2. Network with other peers and schools
3. Engage in continuing professional learning
4. Become more student-centred
5. Initiate greater information and communication technology use in instruction
6. Create better lesson plans
7. Acquire a better understanding of school culture and context and their impact on teaching and learning

These practices relate to cognitive flexibility (Spiro et al. 1995; Spiro and Jehng 1990), which is an indication of successful transfer of learning. Nevertheless, when examined more deeply, even though, for example, graduates were committed to a more student-centred approach, their efforts did not indicate an approach that facilitated student empowerment and deep learning. For example, graduates were not observed to incorporate problem-based learning, whereby students design projects to solve problems, which enhances their higher-order level thinking skills, research skills, communication, creativity and collaboration. Thus, while graduates seem to adopt a philosophy of student-centredness, some of the necessary twenty-first-century learning activities necessary to develop their students into independent thinkers, problem-solvers and learners were not evident. Further, on the point of student-centredness, it should be noted that graduates did not seem to demonstrate intentional planning for differentiated learning classrooms consistently. As such, graduates have not demonstrated that they are concerned with meeting the needs of individual students and improving students' self-efficacy, as espoused by Schoen and Teddlie (2008).

Notwithstanding the apparent shortfall in graduates' practice of the facilitation of deep learning, as espoused by Hattie (2012), the synthesis across the three subject cases does show that according to the Australian DET where the leadership is facilitating and professional learning is encouraged (Australia Victoria DET 2005), teachers can collaborate and innovate, and this was seen among the educational administration graduates. Through clinical supervision, for example, graduates were able to directly influence the quality of teaching and learning in their schools, in ways in which perhaps the other subject teachers were not able to, since they had not been exposed to theories and principles of leadership on their DipEd programme. Perhaps this could be seen as a contributor to the upskilling and reskilling to which the OECD (2019) referred. Further, Darling-Hammond (2010, 35) states, "the advantages gained from effective early interventions are best sustained when they are followed by continued high-quality learning experiences". It seems that this synthesis implies the necessity for continuing professional learning post-initial preparation to buttress teachers' skills and provide them with the opportunities for lifelong learning (Mackenzie 2006). It begs the question of whether the DipEd provider should routinely offer short programmes to "top up" the skills of graduates. Further, one might consider if these programmes should be done in partnership with the schools and even other stakeholders or what the configuration of lifelong learning should look like – should it be a combination of individual and collective approaches and who decides. Chapter 6 of this book provides a deeper expositions on these issues.

References

Australia Victoria DET (Department of Education & Training). 2005. *Professional Learning in Effective Schools: The Seven Principles of Highly Effective Professional Learning*. Melbourne: Victoria Department of Education & Training. https://www.education.vic.gov.au/Documents/school/teachers/profdev/proflearningeffectivesch.pdf.

Darling-Hammond, Linda. 2010. *The Flat World and Education: How America's Commitment to Equity Will Determine Our Future*. New York: Teachers College Press.

Hattie, John. 2012. *Visible Learning for Teachers: Maximizing Impact on Teachers*. London: Routledge.

Herbert, Susan, Jennifer Yamin-Ali, and Shahiba Ali. 2015. *The In-Service Postgraduate Diploma in Education Programme: Consensus and Divergence between Client and Provider: Developing an Agenda for Negotiation*. St Augustine, Trinidad and Tobago: School of Education, The University of the West Indies.

OECD (Organisation for Economic Co-operation and Development). 2019. *OECD Skills Strategy 2019: Skills to Shape a Better Future*. Paris: OECD Publishing. https://doi.org/10.1787/9789264313835-en.

Prosser, Jon. 1999. "The Evolution of School Culture Research." In *School Culture*, edited by Jon Prosser, 1–14. Thousand Oaks, CA: SAGE.

Schoen, La Tefy, and Charles Teddlie. 2008. "A New Model of School Culture: A Response to a Call for Conceptual Clarity." *School Effectiveness and School Improvement* 19 (2): 129–53.

Spiro, Rand J., Paul J. Feltovich, Michael J. Jacobson, and Richard L. Coulson. 1995. "Cognitive Flexibility, Constructivism, and Hypertext: Random Access Instruction for Advanced Knowledge in Ill-Stuctured Domains. *Educational Technology* 31 (5): 24–33.

Spiro, Rand J., and Jihn-Chang Jehng. 1990. "Cognitive Flexibility and Hypertext: Theory and Technology for the Nonlinear and Multidimensional Traversal of Complex Subject Matter." In *Cognition, Education, and Multimedia: Exploring Ideas in High Technology*, edited by D. Nix and Rand J. Spiro, 163–205. Mahwah, NJ: Lawrence Erlbaum Associates.

3. Factors Facilitating the Transfer of Learning and Sustaining Effective Practice

Introduction

Firestone and Pennell in 1993 (quoted in de Comarmond, Abbiss and Lovett 2016) proffered the view that teacher commitment has been a major factor in performance that contributes to quality and success in education and includes the idea that "committed teachers are seen to be those with strong psychological ties to their schools, to their students and to their subject areas" (89). A study conducted by Nias in 1989 (quoted in de Comarmond, Abbiss and Lovett 2016) found that some British primary schoolteachers saw committed practitioners in the field as being "caring and dedicated" as opposed to those who put their own interest first. Yet commitment is but one factor that might facilitate transfer of learning. Trainee motivation (Tziner, Haccoun and Kadish 1991) and trainee locus of control (Noe 1986) also facilitate the transfer of skills to the work environment. In addition to these disparate factors, Baldwin and Ford (1988) identify specific linkages that are key to understanding the transfer process. Learning and retention, which they view as training outcomes, are impacted by training design, trainee characteristics, and work environment characteristics. They offer the hypothesis that trainee characteristics and work-environment characteristics have direct effects on transfer, regardless of initial learning during the training programme or retention of the training material. Baldwin and Ford (1988) support the notion that work environment factors, such as managerial support, transfer climate and opportunity to use trained skills on the job, do influence transfer; but they also recognize the multidimensional nature of these factors, which they feel need to be operationalized in order to establish causality between work-environment factors and behavioural changes.

The DipEd programme introduces and promotes new ways of thinking about teaching and learning to in-service secondary teachers. These new ways are rooted in research and contemporary theories about teaching and learning, which, if adopted, are expected to improve the conditions of and outputs of teaching and learning. Both programme providers and programme sponsors share a common desire for sustainability as an ultimate goal. It is therefore inevitable that teachers' reversion to methods used prior to exposure to the programme is considered a negative outcome. However, while there are many conditions that facilitate sustainability as cited above, in Trinidad and Tobago stakeholders typically assign blame for the lack of sustainability solely on the programme – its content, structure and delivery (James et al. 2013; Ali et al. 2012). The cases below illustrate the factors within the school contexts that facilitated graduates' transfer of learning and sustainability of effective practice.

> **CASE: EDUCATIONAL ADMINISTRATION**
>
> The factors that facilitated graduates applying the theories and principles they are exposed to in the DipEd programme were classified as "school factors" and "personal factors", which are self-explanatory. Deeper expositions on this follow.

School Factors

Three categories of school factors emerged: leadership, infrastructure and school culture.

Leadership

Firstly, there was the leadership aspect, in terms of the principal's intervention by assigning roles to the graduate based on the expertise that the principal felt the participant had gained from being involved in the DipEd. Alicia stated, "I would be encouraged by just the fact that the principal will give you a role. You appreciate that the person [the principal] accepts and acknowledges that you have some skills that they can use." Bernadine referred to leadership similarly as Alicia, in the sense that the leadership at her school allowed for what she called "the flexibility of practice", meaning that she was allowed and supported to implement new ideas that she had learned in the DipEd programme. Additionally, Bernadine indicated that the organizational arrangements at her school, such as the practice of clinical supervision, facilitated her applying the theories and principles that she had learned in the programme to her practice at school.

Infrastructure

The availability of infrastructural facilities enabled teachers to transfer some of the theories and principles learned on the programme into their practice. For example, both Bernadine and Cassian referred to multimedia projectors for use with PowerPoint presentations, and Cassian mentioned the availability of laboratory apparatus and materials. Cassian said "availability of laboratory apparatus and materials and access to multimedia" facilitated the transfer of learning from the programme to her practice. Further, Cassian identified some theories and principles that she was able to implement in her practice as "teaching/learning strategies such as collaboration, inquiry-based learning, problem-based learning, peer assessment, theory of multiple intelligences".

School Culture

Aspects of graduates' school culture also facilitated participants applying theories and principles, which they had learnt in the DipEd programme. Alicia, in her reference to the principal acknowledging her skills and therefore creating opportunities for her to use such skills, speaks to a culture of distributive leadership, whereby leadership is the domain of the many rather than the few. Bernadine spoke of the "ethos", of the fact that "you know there is clinical supervision. It encourages. I would say it motivates, but encourages you as a teacher to keep improving your practice".

Personal Factors

Alicia provided data that fitted into this category. She indicated that her own research done online through her subscriptions to educational sites and her membership in professional educational organizations, such as the Association for Supervision and Curriculum Development (ASCD), facilitated her application of theories and principles learnt from being exposed to the DipEd programme. Bernadine said that she was "motivated to work with the students to ensure that they achieved ... also if I can help the teachers to do better, that is what I do". Cassian referred to herself as "a leader", although she did not hold a formal leadership position in her school. Both Bernadine and Cassian eventually did master's programmes. Graduates' personal desire to improve themselves professionally and, as a corollary, their work environments also facilitated the implementation of the theories and principles they learned in the DipEd programme in their practice.

Discussion

The analysis of those data on the factors that facilitated graduates implementing theories and principles that they learned in the DipEd programme in their practice shows that the culture that existed in the schools was a huge driver. Specifically, the model of culture espoused by Schoen and Teddlie (2008), with its four dimensions, namely: professional orientation, organizational structure, quality of the learning environment and student-centred focus, applies. In terms of "Professional Orientation", among graduates there was a culture that promoted continuing professional learning to improve student learning. Additionally, all three graduates were motivated to improve their practice and did so through pursuing master's degrees, in the case of Cassian and Bernadine, and membership in educational professional organizations, in the case of Alicia. These examples show the graduates' level of professionalism. In terms of a dimension of the "Organizational Structure", the analysis showed that the leadership at the schools was "flexible" enough to allow graduates who held formal positions the opportunities to use the theories and principles that they learned in the DipEd programme to improve teaching and learning. Further, the schools' policies, process, communication and such also facilitated the transfer of graduates' learning into their practice. Still further, Schoen and Teddlie's (2008) dimension of culture that relates to the "Quality of the Learning Environment" is relevant in the cases of Bernadine and Cassian, particularly in the area of infrastructure. The theories and principles which Cassian stated she was able to use in her practice in school have a "student-centred focus" and can improve student learning.

That these four dimensions of the Schoen and Teddlie (2008) model were evident at the schools of all three educational administration cases fits with the categorization of "Generic Culture" of Prosser (1999) that speaks to similarities that exist across different schools.

REFLECTION

These findings show that even in circumstances where the school culture and context facilitate practitioners applying the theories and principles they have learnt during professional learning, the practitioner's intrinsic motivation, personal desire for learning and growing is an important factor because the extent to which the practitioner implements new approaches is determined by his/her knowledge and beliefs.

Questions to Discuss – Educational Administration

1. What factors in your school facilitate your use of the skills and knowledge gained on a professional learning programme?
2. What can you learn from the experiences of these practitioners to ensure that you sustain effective practice post professional learning?
3. What policies can schools institute to support and sustain graduates' effective practice?

CASE: FOREIGN LANGUAGE

Of the four schools examined in this research, it was notable that teachers in the two that were not totally government-owned highlighted many more factors that facilitated them in sustaining effective practice in the teaching of foreign language and in their wider professional practice as a teacher. There emerged four major categories of facilitating factors: DipEd programme content, school factors, personal factors and external factors. Of extreme interest is the declaration of one teacher in a government school that there was nothing in her school that facilitated her effective practice.

DipEd Programme Content

Content that the teachers were exposed to in the DipEd programme remained with them and facilitated effective practice in some ways. Learning from peers, structuring a lesson, learning from classroom research, the use of a set induction, infusing context, collaboration and student-centred teaching were all emphasized as main elements in the DipEd programme.

Brenda said that her decision to change her approach to teaching was because of the DipEd. She explained: "I saw different methods that you could use... from other teachers and from what we were learning on the course...and I tried it." She also indicated that when planning lessons, in order to enable her students to relate to the content, "I think about real life. When would they have a chance to use this? And then I try to devise or maybe bring that area in the classroom...even if it is like a situation and we are doing written work, it's a situational um...scenario that I give them." In the programme, there was an emphasis on the infusion of context in the teaching of the foreign language, which clearly impacted Brenda's teaching. She used this approach to reach her students. The research, which she conducted while in the programme, was on "moving from oral work into written work". She commented as follows:

> I still use it today to get them to write...I do a lot of oral practice...and role-play, so once they can say it, they can act it out, they could bring it back to me...it's easy for them when it comes to writing. So, I still use it...I still do the peer correction and I still do the...the brainstorming...I still put up, like if they write a sentence and it's not correct, I put it up on the board, let them see it and then I ask them...'But what is wrong here?'...I still do all of that.

Any success that Dana experienced in her teaching post DipEd, she said, came from some aspects of the programme: "When I did the DipEd, I was teaching only four years...and I realized I needed to learn how to actually structure a class.

I didn't know how to really plan a class, so that has certainly helped me now in how to...structure a class. Also, in terms of strategies and exercises and thing, you know?" Two elements which were main features of the programme were evident in the lessons observed. One was the effective use of a set induction, where the context set enabled students to be on task, and the other was the use of the linguistic function to guide the production of the language, as opposed to the encouragement of translation.

Celia declared that two areas of learning in the programme had a strong influence on her teaching: "I definitely think the context, teaching in context, was a big eye-opener in the DipEd... and so that has definitely been something I continued...as well as collaboration...with some of the teachers who would have been on DipEd with me. We still communicate. We have...there's a teachers' 'Frenchbook' on Facebook that shares strategies...."

One of Anthony's lessons observed started with a rich context which drove the lesson. He explained after the lesson:

> Well, one thing I actually learnt in DipEd that stuck with me throughout, was teaching in context...and I say to my younger colleagues all the time you can't just go into the classroom and just deliver something. You have to create some kind of context for the students to be able to understand what you're saying and a deep context too...But that part for me, on the DipEd programme, apart from how you structure your lesson, the activities you use within the lesson and then how you evaluate. Those have stayed with me throughout from what I've learnt in the programme.

Student-centred teaching is promoted in the DipEd programme. There was evidence that Anthony's lessons are student-centred. He elaborated on this learning: "I would say that they're student-centred because there are ample opportunities for the students to engage in the material, for example, the class we were having a while ago, the students were engaging with the materials. I merely provided. I built it on what they knew."

School Factors

Encouragement by Administration

There were a variety of ways identified in which the school's administration facilitated teachers' effective practice, whether it was through systems, policies or the principal's disposition. Celia highlighted the structure of the department as a definite advantage. She explained: "With the HoD, we have the performance management system in place...ever so often the HoD would come and check our classes. She would actually sit in our classes to see how things are going, as well as we have weekly departmental meetings, and I think that helps." Anthony highlighted "encouragement by the HoD...to focus on different [linguistic] skills..." as a fillip to his teaching.

A principal who was "very facilitating and encouraging" was an enabler for Brenda to sustain effective practice in her foreign language teaching. Opportunity to explore and expand teachers' thinking and functioning was cited as a facilitator for effective practice. Anthony, for example, said he was "given room to expand possibilities" by designing "new teaching materials for use by all – a booklet for forms 1–5 – to enable students to explore the material before and after class to enable smooth flow for thematic teaching". This included the extended activity of "doing surveys to determine results of the booklet effort". In addition, the policy of this school was that every student studied foreign language up to year five, which could be seen as a motivating factor for students. Administrative support enabled Celia to promote language learning outside of the classroom walls through projects like a "trip to Martinique" and *"Tour de Trincity"*, which is a mock *"Tour de France"* where students of French operate in their own school vicinity to interact with the neighbourhood in French. Communication systems facilitated by the principal of Celia's school made sharing ideas and gaining approval for plans and projects easy since he practised an open-door policy.

Functioning Department

Effective practice was sustained in two of the four schools through the professional functioning of the foreign language (FL) department. Anthony always used "we" when he spoke of his work in the school: "All of us work together...it's always a collaborative effort...we always talk about how we can do better, create a better environment for our students... sometimes on the phone up to midnight." Celia described the FL department in her school as "pretty close, so that helps" and added that "there's a lot of sharing".

While Brenda and Dana did not seem to be supported as effectively in their departments, it appears they originally had the will and inclination to help members of their department to function effectively. Brenda reports: "In the past, ... when I had now come out fresh from DipEd... I had little staff meetings. At that time, I assumed acting HoD...and I had little staff meetings for the group...to show them my lesson plans and what we could do and discussions..."; and Dana who acted as HoD for a short while said: "I would sit in on their class and that sort of thing...most of them the classes weren't structured...I went through the format that I used when I did DipEd. And...some of them they tried to do it."

Availability of Technology Resources

The DipEd programme included a module on technology integration for all areas of specialization. The programme encouraged student teachers to use technology in a variety of ways for delivering the curriculum. Two of the four foreign language teachers used the multimedia projector for delivery. The effective use of technology was evident in Celia's practice. She used a video of French students discussing school routine and presented electronic graphics with accompanying vocabulary. She also used technology, via the projector and a screen in place of handouts. She indicated: "The school is big on technology" and "we have a computer in our classroom which helps." This approach regarding the use of technology in teaching is clearly the position of the school's administration. Anthony's department is keen on using technology to enhance the development of linguistic skills. "For listening practice," he said, "we also create material because we have the software, where we could actually create this. It's called Text Aloud. We can actually create audio material." Again, this is not just on an individual level, but on a departmental level. On an individual level, he manifested the use of still graphics on a whiteboard accompanied by vocabulary.

While they did not use electronic media, Dana used picture charts with accompanying vocabulary, and Brenda used the whiteboard to draw a family of vocabulary and phrases. They used what they had access to.

Personal Factors

The personal factors which propelled teachers to sustain effective practice were their philosophy, their passion for teaching and what that entails, and their own commitment to learning.

Personal Beliefs and Characteristics

The personal beliefs and characteristics of each of these teachers act as key facilitators in their efforts to sustain their effectiveness as foreign language teachers.

Anthony believed in "creating a very student-centred environment in which students are comfortable with what they learn...preparing students to contribute positively to society and make a difference". His belief was that "students have potential for greatness". His vision of his own work is that it should "impact wider than his school". As such, he was at the time of the conduct of this research, heavily involved in a modern language organization at the executive level. In that capacity, he organized educational trips and Spelling Bees for schools beyond his own, and he and teachers in that organization were "always planning to refine our skills as teachers". His beliefs about foreign language learning impacted the way he functioned in the school. He stated the following:

> When we were told it was mandatory that all students would do a foreign language, I was of the view that students should be encouraged to…my argument did not come across well to those in authority…so I started to do things differently…I started to encourage my colleagues to reorient their thoughts about how we deliver the curriculum from the first form… we are always working along with the other two teachers to ensure that at the end of the First Form students develop an appreciation of the language.

Celia's belief in the importance of developing the whole child is manifested in her activities outside of delivering the formal curriculum. According to her principal, she "has been an excellent member of staff. She's not one of those teachers who is limited to her classes, her subject area." He corroborated facts about her involvement in helping students who needed support for school supplies or school-related needs. Brenda stated, "I believe that every child can learn, but we need to adopt different approaches to get to them." This belief drives her to cater to her students in ways that would motivate them and help them learn. Her HoD said, "She uses a lot of, plenty plenty *(sic)* activities and her class is always noisy…constructive noise." This aligns with Brenda's indication that she uses a lot of rhythm in her classes, with students drumming and thumping their feet. She explains: "I make adjustments. I do what I *can* do…in the classroom with the children…because you don't always need technology to…to deliver in the classroom…and so whatever I can do, because my kids learn best with rhythm. They love it. It's easy to get them to do the work with rhythm so you do…whatever we can do, we do…so a lot of singing, chanting, role-playing or to act."

Despite the constraints that Dana had mentioned about her students' behaviour and learning difficulties, her belief that students must be afforded the opportunity to grow academically pervaded her overall practice, as evidenced in her principal's words: "She is very diligent...I find that she puts a lot into her work...right now she wants to do A level Spanish. She comes and she says, 'Miss, when we go across to the new school, we going to get, we're going to introduce the A Levels?'" Clearly, Dana sees the potential in students to achieve more and is desirous of providing them with the opportunity to do so.

Passion for Teaching

Passion for teaching is a characteristic that facilitated graduates' effective practice post DipEd. It is evident that Anthony is, indeed, passionate about teaching, which he views in a totally holistic way. His HoD described the evidence of his passion in this way:

> [Anthony] is one of those experts in...curriculum...because he's very organized, rushing round so that...it's easy to pick his brain and then most people trust him...He has already created a reputation among students of himself...so even the most difficult parent could totally...accept what he recommends and then work with him and so much so that he started a Spanish group, and even people who we know could not get in tried to get in and tried to get those grades to get in. Parents begging...He is one of the major players in the Language Day...Right now they're trying to do a brand thing to get more funding, and he's the one that we will go to...He wanted to do a staff orientation for the staff, new people...we have the people who have not been having as much success leading their classes, and he was able to talk about transactions and bringing this to the table. It did have an impact...And he manages to do these things without ever wanting to be...to be thanked....

Celia describes herself as being "into school". She believes teaching to be "beyond just sharing of the curriculum. I think it's about sharing...making sure values are implanted so that when the students leave here, they can actually create a positive environment wherever they are...So I think relationships are definitely important, between the students and the teachers, creating relationships among students, and traditional things like respect."

This belief translates into certain effective teacher behaviours: "I tend to ask my students a lot about how they feel. I try to be in touch with them. So, I try to use stuff that I know would impact them...the choice of topics would always be along that line and I also try to feel them out...If I find they're not getting along, I'll usually ask them to tell me what the problem is."

Brenda believed in "trying to reach as many children as I possibly can". According to her, she designs her learning activities to suit the students' learning styles and preferences. In the case of Dana, like Celia, teaching went beyond delivering the formal curriculum. From Dana's description of her work, it was evident that preparing students to function socially superseded the teaching of the foreign language. She described her students as having learning disabilities and being socially disadvantaged generally. As such, she sees her role as "broader than foreign language teacher". In this regard, Dana is, in effect, sustaining effective holistic practice as a teacher. She said: "It's also not just about teaching a subject...in the schools I have worked at. It's much, much, much more than just teaching Spanish...you teach all sorts of things, about life, manners. Sometimes that takes up more time than actually teaching the subject...I also had to deal with many other issues apart from teaching Spanish." This is a professional decision which Dana had to make considering her teaching context.

Commitment to Learning

It was through his commitment to learning through additional graduate studies in education that Anthony could engage in further reflection so that he creates a learning context "where the student is learning to fix a problem or address an issue...not just fit in the status quo, not just fit in...really to make a difference". Celia also continued on her professional learning journey and enrolled in a master's programme post DipEd, and she demonstrated a commitment to her colleagues' learning by actively sharing her own knowledge and expertise within her department, especially concerning technology use.

External Factor

Curriculum Division of the Ministry of Education

What two teachers cited as helpful were the resources available to them through the Curriculum Division of the Ministry of Education. Anthony was of the view that the National Curriculum for Spanish was a useful guide for the department's planning: "The thing about the Spanish, the national curriculum...is that it is outlined, within the curriculum, what the objectives would be....and well, everything is there, the cultural element is there...and the topic is there. For us, we just make some internal adjustments because sometimes we realize our students can go a bit faster...." Brenda indicated: "I use what we get from the curriculum. They have a nice package now. NCSE [National Certificate of Secondary Education] has given us a nice package with lesson planning and ideas... not only the lesson plan itself but what you can use in [the lesson]."

The blend of DipEd programme content, school, personal and external factors, in varying degrees in the case of each teacher, was a positive indicator that these teachers do have some support for sustaining effective practice and also have the will to engage in it.

Discussion

School culture was a definite contributor to teachers' ability or inability to sustain effective practice. Where the culture was positive, it was the organizational structure as described by Schoen and Teddlie (2008), for example, departmental meetings or open-door policy for communication with administration, or the facilitation of a learning environment, that was conducive to a student-oriented focus. Encouragement by administration, a functioning department and the provision of and encouragement to use technology were features of the organizational structure and the quality of the learning environment. The teachers' personal beliefs, passion for teaching and commitment to learning enhanced the professional orientation of the school. In two of the more "organized schools", the "perceived culture" (Prosser 1999) is a factor which probably contributes to the success of the school through parent and community support. In those two schools also, their "unique culture" (Prosser 1999) is also an enabling factor, almost a self-fulfilling prophecy, with strong positive and enduring values which guide their policies and overall mores.

REFLECTION

As expected, programme content, systemic and personal factors facilitated teachers' ability to sustain effective practice. The role of the school's administration clearly impacted teacher output in not only providing adequate facilities and ensuring that structures are functioning but also by the administration's willingness and ability to encourage effective practice.

The wider systemic support, such as the Ministry of Education, is also seen to be of significant relevance to teachers' work and disposition. A key factor emerging in the issue of effective practice is "the teacher as a person". It is the disposition that teachers bring to their practice that might ultimately empower them to be effective.

> **Questions to Discuss – Foreign Language**
> 1. What lessons would you draw from these teachers' ability to sustain effective teaching practice?
> 2. What would facilitate your implementation of the lessons mentioned in question one?
> 3. In what ways do you see your own beliefs about teaching reflected in any of the four foreign language teachers, and how are those beliefs translated into effective practice in your context?

> **CASE: SCIENCE**
> The factors which facilitated the use of theories and principles were categorized as school factors such as school culture (organizational structure, including school leadership; beliefs and practices as reflected in school policies and processes and practices; quality of the learning environment and student-centred focus); school resources (physical and human) and space; student factors related to student characteristics and abilities; teacher factors such as the characteristics of the teachers; the alignment of the DipEd programme with the school context; and external factors such as input from external stakeholders (MoE, the Caribbean Examinations Council (CXC), parents).

School Factors
Organizational Structure and School Leadership

The organizational structure and leadership can facilitate DipEd science graduates' application of theories and principles to which they were exposed in the DipEd programme. The school leadership is vested in the principal, with leadership assistance from the vice principal and from middle management, such as deans and heads, comprising the executive management team. Although not necessarily formally appointed as HoDs and deans by the MoE, at all four schools, an organizational structure of subject departments, led by a head of department, and deans of discipline existed. Two of the science graduates who participated in this research often unofficially performed the functions associated with these leadership roles.

Principals play a key role in establishing and maintaining the professional culture of a school, which is a manifestation of their philosophy of education. From professional development plans to the implementation of clinical supervision and professional learning sessions on classroom management, the principal helps to create an ethos that facilitates teaching and learning and hence supports the application of the principles and theories to which DipEd students were exposed. At the time of the interview with principals, two of them indicated that professional learning sessions had been scheduled for the upcoming week. For example, Principal 1 indicated that she had begun on-site training sessions for new staff in classroom management issues. At this school, the school finances as necessary individual staff participation in professional learning activities, which are held frequently. Most of the staff members have completed the DipEd, and there is often a period of waiting before new teachers can apply to the programme.

Wilhelminah also mentioned the principal's attention to professional learning. "The principal plans for professional development. She realizes that new teachers need assistance... We did a staff development for that [formative assessment] too.... 'cause she [the principal] was saying make sure to give practice before the test...What the principal is doing, because she realizes new teachers need assistance...she is doing some type of training in classroom management."

Principal 4 provided similar information as Principal 1. She stated: "Professional development [occurs] once per term. One tomorrow is entitled 'Educating with Technology:

Empowerment through Instructional Technology.'"
Caribbean Secondary Education Certificate (CSEC) Math and English examination days are used to meet and discuss as well as the first two days in September. At another school, Principal 2 indicated that a "professional development workshop is presently being planned with a focus on building capacity in a professional learning environment, which is meant to focus the staff on their critical role in implementing the School Development Plan 2014-2017".

Some schools have policies and processes which align with ideas promoted in the DipEd programme and hence provide an environment in which ideas introduced in the programme are sustained. These include the practice of clinical supervision, implementation of an ICT policy, and practices such as scheduled departmental meetings, relationships among staff and Open Day events for the general public. Deeper expositions on these follow.

Clinical Supervision

At three of the four schools, there was an entrenched system of clinical supervision. The HoD and principal visited classrooms regularly, and teachers were therefore required to engage in formal lesson planning and to submit written plans, activities which are introduced in the DipEd programme. According to Wilhelminah, "...the lesson planning and the practice of doing it, the clinical supervision, I think it makes you better, yes, people quarrel about it, but I think it makes you a better teacher. Because you actually sit down and think about how you are going from stage A to stage B, and with that, it is a plus."

The culture of lesson planning and attempts to establish a culture of mentorship were also evident in Wilhelmina's comment: "Because remember she (the HoD) has a file on everybody. If a senior teacher is uncooperative, you simply copy some lesson plans and give it to the teacher to go through." A similar approach was noted at School 2, this time regarding the use of contemporary assessment approaches, which supports the activities and ideas proposed in the DipEd programme. Sophia stated: "It was mentioned in the School Development Plans. At least teachers should be using two different types of assessment throughout the term." At School 4, both principal and teacher (Peter) mentioned the frequent use of clinical supervision. For example, the principal stated: "At the start of every term, HoDs submit schemes of work across the year groups, which are standardized. Clinical supervision is scheduled. HoDs plan ahead for teachers to be visited with the six-day cycle." The principal elaborated. "At the start of the school year, the HoD has discussions in advance [of classroom observations]...teachers identify weaknesses and the HoD [identifies] other areas that need attention. [They are] looked at for growth and development. Every term there is clinical supervision with fourteen per department."

Schools with entrenched systems of clinical supervision are more likely to facilitate the application of principles and theories introduced in the DipEd programme, for example, the importance of preparing written lesson plans as contributing to effective practice. At these three schools (two five-year government and one seven-year government assisted), full written lesson plans were available for classroom observations.

ICT Policy

The developments in ICT are introduced in the DipEd programme, and teachers in the programme are encouraged to develop technology, pedagogy and content knowledge (TPACK). Wilhelminah mentioned that the school's ICT policies play a role in determining whether teachers can infuse technology in their lessons: "So I think with the technology, [Form 6] are allowed their phones, not the lower school, so I have to copy it for the lower school." While Peter indicated his interest in technology use: "I am interested in leveraging web technology. So I am interested in open-source learning as a tool to enhance the teaching and learning process here." Peter's principal corroborated Peter's interest in and use of technology and indirectly revealed the school's support for technology use: "Those who have done the DipEd are ahead and use technology for engagement."

Departmental Meetings

At some schools, there are efforts to develop certain minimum standards of operation. Accordingly, there are formal opportunities for science teachers to meet, collaborate and engage and discuss issues within the school day. There are scheduled departmental meetings, which is a mechanism for developing a learning community within the department. During these meetings, teachers share ideas with less experienced colleagues and hence dissemination of ideas introduced in the DipEd programme is facilitated. Wilhelminah states: "Everything is standardized. And they encourage you now when we have departmental meeting...Every Monday. Every single week. It's not a free period."

Practices
Relationships among Staff

Teachers at the four schools indicated there are collegial relationships among staff and that with student learning as the focus of their practice, there is informal and formal sharing of strategies that facilitate student learning. Accordingly, some ideas and strategies introduced in the DipEd programme are disseminated. The support of the HoD also facilitates communication among staff and adoption of these strategies. For example, Wilhelminah stated:

> We collaborate in terms of the different techniques we might use to help students understand...DipEd graduates work with new teachers. ...Show her how to do tests, how to teach lessons. The senior teachers help the junior ones. She comes to me to see where we are in the scheme of work and I tell her

"Well, you can borrow my notes", and I told her how I did the demonstration. She likes to do new things. Whatever new ideas we bring up, she (the HoD) is supportive. She likes to implement new things. So, I have to say, very collaborative.

Sophia's experience was similar. She said:

A lot of times what I try to do is I would liaise with the other teachers who probably teaching…you know. It may be two of us teaching Forms 1…The other chem teacher, she would have been pretty new, junior to me…and I would have found some nice activities to use in a lesson, and I would share with her… from time she would come, you know, "I want you to help me to work out this…SBAs are due…I had a teacher look at it, and I had my technician here do all sorts of things and eventually between the two of them they came up with a contraption."

Showcasing Students' Work

Educators at two seven-year secondary schools reported events that allowed students to showcase their understanding of science. The events were the annual Open Day session and the annual science fair. The Open Day was organized to promote a positive image of the school, and primary-aged schoolchildren within the district are invited. The secondary students act as hosts and are required to plan for and participate in science activities. In preparing for this activity, the secondary students engage in the deep and meaningful learning required to engage with and interest the young audience. The activity also facilitates the development of twenty-first-century skills of communication, collaboration and creative thinking. Accordingly, many of the principles promoted in the DipEd programme are applied when the host students are involved in the Open Day activities. Wilhelminah explains, "I think she [the principal] wants to encourage people to come here because she wants it to be a first-choice school." She elaborates: "An Open Day is to get students from primary schools to come here so they would choose the school. So, her idea of Open Day is to use students and teachers to explain. We are like tour guides.

They actually schedule schools and, for chemistry, we do a lab demonstration…So our students get a little more excited about the science. I prepare my students. They demonstrate for me prior to the actual day so they have confidence." Principal 4 described Peter's involvement in preparing students for the science fair. She said: "Every year we have a science fair. Students enter. The teacher leads by example. He encourages them."

School Resources: Technical Support and Resources

For science teachers, practical work is an integral component of science teaching and learning. Practical work allows students to engage in the learning process through hands-on, minds-on activities. Teachers in the DipEd programme are introduced to these learning principles. The principal's leadership and support and the level of collegiality and collaboration among staff ensure learning is facilitated through opportunities for inquiry through practical work. Three of the four teachers referred to the availability of materials and technical support personnel required to assist with the practical investigative component of the science curriculum. For example, in reference to availability of materials for lab work, Wilhelminah said, "…and the lab tech, if there is no material for a demonstration, she will order it. Once we have the money, she would say: 'What do you need?'"

Sophia appreciated a renovated lab space: "I was very much impressed when we returned to school (after the July/August) and saw she [the principal] did over the cupboards… they are very nice with our department. I think the majority of the vote is actually spent on science material." Mahalia introduced students to the dedicated space for laboratory work and co-opted the laboratory technician to lead a session on the importance of safety in the laboratory: "At the start of the first term, we would bring them to see the lab, what a lab looks like and the lab tech would talk to them about safety that kind of thing."

Student Factors

The students' response to teachers' approaches to and strategies for teaching/learning science provides the impetus for teachers to persevere with and hence to sustain the student-centred approaches, including the application of TPCK, to which they have been exposed in the programme. Mahalia referred to the students' enthusiasm and their desire for a total experience when required to organize their student presentations and that their technical capabilities surpassed her expectations: "When they had their presentations, they even wanted to have refreshments after. So it was fun for them...But teaching boy children – they shock you [in terms of their competencies with technology]." Wilhelminah also commented on the students' ICT prowess: "I give them my original and they make it. For the Form 6, they are technical, they would snap it, scan it, put it on the computer. The Form 6, they are good."

Teacher Factors
Efficacy with Selected Strategies

Teachers' confidence and competence in using interactive student-centred strategies play a role in sustaining the use of these strategies. A positive student response bolstered teacher confidence. For example, Wilhelminah was pleased with students' projects as an outcome of project-based learning and thus was encouraged to continue its use:

> Yes, Multiple Intelligences. And that is when we started to let the students do projects...we had them bring in materials and had them actually build models of the cell...In Form 3, we also had a nice, a fantastic project on the planets and what the surface was made of. Oh, my God, that thing was beautiful! That was amazing. Students got a binder and for each planet surface, they got material...If you see how beautiful that was.

So what you can say is that we encourage the children to do more projects.

Teachers' Beliefs and Characteristics

Teachers' perspectives play a significant role in terms of their tenacity to try new strategies in the teaching context. Teachers with a high internal locus of control and strong belief that the practices to which they are exposed are valuable seem to sustain the practices to which they have been exposed, regardless of the context to which they return. Wilhelminah and Peter illustrate.

Wilhelminah had a well-defined moral purpose for teaching, that is, improved student learning which impacted the strategies adopted in the classroom: "If you want the children to learn better, you can't just stand up in front of the class and talk...If you have a computer, they have pictures...."

Teachers' propensity for reflection also facilitates continuous improvement and sustains effective practice. Developing the reflective habit is a cornerstone of the DipEd programme. Engaging in reflection led to dissatisfaction with less than their best for each child, which propelled graduates to find ways to improve their practice. For example, Wilhelminah analysed student performance data to determine the changes required at the individual student level: "I would notice well that this child did well in coursework but not in end-of-term. And I think we have to reflect on what we did in the last term, and we modify it. So I think we go back and look and reflect."

Peter's disposition for lifelong learning and his belief that the reality of the teaching context should not constrain his attempts to provide the best for his charges impact his actions in the school setting. He stated the following:

> The truth be told I generally don't believe that there is any excuse to reverting to old ways of teaching. It does not matter what your context is, you could apply some of the new knowledge and skills from the DipEd.... I genuinely believe that. When I came away from DipEd, it wasn't you could only

teach if the conditions were ideal.... Well, it's that I am an eternal student. I believe that teacher is first a student, and a student doesn't learn unless he puts into practice, and I am on a path as long as I live to improve myself. And if I am in an environment where I am improving myself then, my improvement would be of nothing unless it radiates out into the environment. I am not here just to run the maze, but I do believe that if everyone had that philosophy, that we would deliver. I am a person once you are alive you are to grow. It is a never-ending growth process.

Peter was committed to student involvement in the learning process. He adopted strategies which facilitated their engagement in the learning process. Consequently, his comments revealed that theories and principles of active learning introduced in the DipEd were sustained:

There are a number of things besides the lab. Since the text book is the centre of the... is really the number one resource in learning, what I try to get the students to do, they can do a number of things, as I had mentioned before. They can do concept identification; they can generate questions without my input; they can summarize the information; they can do concept mapping. In addition to that, they can do problems posed to them. All of this without a lecture being presented. So I could tell you OK, read section 1 of chapter 4 and present a problem based on the information there.

The DipEd Programme Content

The teachers also referred to aspects of the DipEd programme itself (the nature of the programme) which facilitated transfer to their practice. For example, they referred to the alignment of the programmatic content with their needs. Teachers appreciated aspects of the programme that aligned with their practical needs. For instance, they found value in aspects like exposure to lesson planning, including components such as set induction to engage students' interest, as well as techniques for involving students through questioning and group-work strategies like Jigsaw. These strategies were particularly helpful in managing the delivery of substantial content within the constraints of limited teaching and learning time. Mahalia's and Peter's comments illustrate.

Mahalia said: "That's what I liked about the DipEd; it showed you about the lesson plan and the set induction. Bloom's taxonomy, that helped me a lot with planning lessons and probably the time management aspect. Jigsaw is a very useful strategy to deliver content." Peter said: "One of the most outstanding things that I took from the DipEd is questioning, the kinds of questions that I ask. If you were to ask what I took away from the DipEd, the questions that I asked at the end was (sic) straight from my DipEd experience. Even the whole aspect of getting the students more involved."

External Factors

External stakeholders, such as parents, often play a role in determining how well the school functions. Students from high socio-economic status (SES) can assist schools by providing resources either through direct monetary donations or indirectly through access to services required. For example, when student-centred approaches are adopted, there is often a need to use activity sheets and worksheets that are copied and provided for groups of students or for individual students. Teachers within schools with resources are better positioned to utilize these strategies more frequently. Further policies from the MoE and the Caribbean Examinations Council (CXC) can provide a policy environment that makes it easy to apply the theories and principles introduced in the DipEd programme. The following excerpts illustrate parental support and the influence of the MoE and CXC.

Parental Impact: SES

In some schools, parents were willing to assist financially to support teaching and learning. Parents' support provided paper and/or access to copiers for production of worksheets/activity sheets. Wilhelminah reports, "I think this year the Form Ones – every child brought in a ream of paper....We would collect money and make the prints or you let students whose parents have access to a copy machine assist...The copy machine has been down for a while, and the children get frustrated. I had to collect money and get it outside."

MoE Policy and CXC Requirements

With directives from the MoE or CXC for use of new technologies and/or approaches to teaching, teachers were less resistant to applying knowledge and competencies gained during delivery of the technology integration module to enhance the teaching/learning experience.

Sophia refers explicitly to MoE policy: "The MoE policy was about ICT and the infusion of that, so one of the things I identified is that ... the teachers should be using more technology."

Mahalia corroborates the role of the MoE, as well as CXC with responsibility for the Caribbean Advanced Proficiency Examination (CAPE), saying "...that what you would call policies and so made at the MoE, how it impacts directly on schools, and things like the CAPE, that these things come. We are not on our own, so it makes me less resistant then. When you hear about change. I know people were quarrelling why it is that you have to do it. The school is not by itself, it's connected."

Discussion

The dimensions of Schoen and Teddlie's (2008) school culture that were most applicable to the factors facilitating the sustainability of effective practice among the science graduates were "professional orientation", "the activities and attitudes that characterize the degree of professionalism present in the faculty"; "organizational structure", "the style of leadership communication and processes that characterize the way the school conducts its business" and "student-centred focus", "the extent to which the needs of individual students are met by the school's programmes, policies, rituals, routines and traditions" (Schoen and Teddlie 2008, 140–41). A positive professional orientation was evident when teachers were concerned about student performance and sought to engage in professional learning either externally or internally through various school-based initiatives to provide the best learning experiences for their students. This professional orientation, when supported by the organizational structure, such as management teams, principal's leadership and vision for the school and the institution of meetings at the departmental level, as well as the adoption of clinical supervision, facilitated the application of theories and principles to which teachers were exposed during the DipEd year. These factors constitute a "generic culture" (Prosser 1999) that has emerged regardless of school type and provides an environment in which theories and principles introduced in the DipEd are facilitated. A significant finding was reference to teachers' reflection on and in action within one school, which translated into a student-centred focus with attention to individual students' needs and abilities as well as the Open Day event – a unique cultural element (Prosser 1999). Other factors that facilitated transfer of knowledge included the student expectations, dimensions of the programme itself and external factors such as parental support, and national and regional educational policies. The external factors comprise aspects of the wider culture (Prosser 1999) that influence the activities of the schools. Knowledge of these factors and cultural dimensions, which promote knowledge transfer, can lead to deliberate actions for sustaining effective practice.

REFLECTION

As a lecturer/tutor in the DipEd programme, it is heartening to discover there are factors within the practice context: school-related factors, including school leadership and organization, and school resources, teacher factors, student factors and factors associated with external stakeholders, as well as the alignment of the programme with teachers' needs, which facilitate the sustainability of ideas introduced to science teachers in the DipEd programme. From a lecturer's perspective, the programme is underpinned by contemporary teaching and learning theories and principles assumed to achieve effective practice. However, teacher education/training programmes are unlikely to succeed without the support and buy-in from stakeholders within the system, as different messages and expectations of teachers will be communicated within the practice context. Clearly, if the ideas promoted in the programme have currency within the system, then the requisite structures, policies, routines and procedures will emerge, facilitating sustainability and promoting best practice outcomes. The findings provide evidence that there is some degree of alignment in thinking and actions among stakeholders in education.

Questions to Discuss – Science

1. Which of the facilitating conditions for student-centred science teaching are part of your school culture?
2. What are your suggestions for school-based professional learning of science teachers to optimize science teaching and learning?
3. What resources do science teachers require to sustain effective practice in schools?

Conclusion

Research in 1996 by Joyce and Weil (quoted in Kain 2003, 15) concludes that "relatively few teachers...will even try a new teaching strategy unless they are provided with a support system...." The role of teacher support is also highlighted by Hirsh (2009) and by Boyd, Szplit and Zbróg (2014) who refer to the need for workplace environments to support trainee teachers and newly trained teachers in their professional growth. Evidently, facilitating factors within the practice context are integral to promoting and sustaining the behaviours of newly trained teachers. Further, the interconnectedness between individual characteristics and the environmental factors in sustaining behaviours is supported by Zaky (2015). Without these facilitators, according to Fullan (2001, 92), the "implementation dip" occurs – a tendency to return to old habits in the face of the hurdles encountered when attempts are made to change behaviours to accommodate new learnings.

The findings from this study revealed evidence of the factors facilitating the transfer of knowledge to practices of selected high-performing graduates within the three specializations: educational administration, foreign languages and science. Common among the three cases were school factors and personal factors. For example, the schools in which administration promoted a culture of leadership and support for professional learning crafted policies which encouraged adopting a culture of high-functioning subject departments across the curriculum areas. These schools also ensured the availability of resources for ICT and for practical work in science. These all act as supports and props for teachers who are exposed to contemporary ideas during their enrolment in the DipEd programme. The department can function as a community of practice (Louis and Marks 1998; Wenger 1998; McLaughlin and Talbert 2006; Stoll and Louis 2007; Timperley et al. 2007; Vescio, Ross and Adams 2008; Pang and Wang 2016; Katz, Earl and Ben

Jaafar 2009; Yamin-Ali 2021), which is in and of itself a vehicle for professional learning. The culture and context of the school therefore matter. When school culture and context are coupled with personal factors, such as teachers who were committed to their own lifelong learning and to using their new-found skills and knowledge in ensuring that their students performed optimally and who are passionate about and committed to learning, then the likelihood of applying educational theories and principles increases. In other words, principles and theories promoted in the programme were sustained where individual characteristics interface with contextual and cultural support.

Unique to the curriculum specializations, graduates also mentioned that aspects of the professional learning programme that were aligned to their lived realities facilitated their sustained use. Fullan (2001) refers to "need" as a driver of change. Programme relevance cannot therefore be overlooked as a significant factor facilitating sustainability. In addition, schools with strong support from external stakeholders, such as parents with financial means, were more likely to plan for student activities which are promoted in the programme and which required a variety of resources. Also, key are external stakeholders, such as the MoE, which can influence teachers' implementation of new ideas, for example, the ICT policy of the MoE, which supports the principles of technology integration promoted in the DipEd programme. The facilitating factors induced in this study align with Fullan's (2001, 72) nine critical interactive factors which affect implementation and which he organized into three main categories. The three categories are "characteristics of the innovation or change project", in this case the theories and principles introduced in the DipEd programme; the "local characteristics", which in this study include the principal and teacher and the "external factors comprising government and other agencies", reflected in this study as agencies such as the MoE and the CXC. Finally, when teachers discerned positive student response to their new behaviours, they were motivated to sustain the changed behaviours introduced when enrolled in the DipEd programme, further evidence of the influence of culture and context on sustaining effective practice.

It is therefore evident that programme developers at the School of Education, UWI and secondary school personnel cannot operate in silos. Continuous dialogue is required for alignment of the professional learning context with the practice contexts and vice versa, to facilitate sustainability.

References

Ali, Shahiba, Désirée Augustin, Susan Herbert, Freddy James, Sharon Phillip, Joycelyn Rampersad, and Jennifer Yamin-Ali. 2012. "Is Anybody Listening? Stakeholders' Perspectives on the In-Service Diploma in Education Programme at the School of Education, The University of the West Indies, St. Augustine Campus." *Caribbean Curriculum* 19:173–96.

Baldwin, Timothy, and J. Kevin Ford. 1988. "Transfer of Training: A Review and Direction for Future Research." *Personnel Psychology* 41 (1): 63–105.

Boyd, Pete, Agnieszka Szplit, and Zuzanna Zbróg. 2014. Introduction to *Teacher Educators And Teachers As Learners: International Perspectives*, edited by Pete Boyd, Agnieszka Szplit, and Zuzanna Zbróg, 7–17. Kraków: Libron.

de Comarmond Odile, Jane Abbiss, and Susan Lovett. 2016. "Commitment Crises: Voices of Secondary Teachers." In *Professional Learning in Education: Challenges for Teacher Educators, Teachers and Student Teachers*, edited by Bram de Wever, Ruben Vanderlinde, Melissa Tuytens, and Antonia Aelterman, 87–111. Ghent, Belgium: Academia Press.

Fullan, Michael. 2001. *The New Meaning of Educational Change*. 3rd ed. New York: Teachers College Press.

Hirsh, Stephanie. 2009. "A New Definition." *Journal of Staff Development* 30 (4): 10–16

James, Freddy., Sharon Phillip, Susan Herbert, Désirée Augustin, Jennifer Yamin-Ali, Shahiba Ali, and Joycelyn Rampersad. 2013. "Is Anybody Listening? Teachers' Views of Their In-Service Diploma in Education Programme." *Caribbean Curriculum* 20:77–100.

Kain, Daniel L. 2003. *Problem-based Learning for Teachers Grades 6–12*. Boston, MA: Pearson Education.

Katz, Steven, Lorna M. Earl, and Sonia Ben Jaafar. 2009. *Building and Connecting Learning Communities: The Power of Networks for School Improvement*. Thousand Oaks, CA: Corwin Press.

Louis, Karen Seashore, and Helen M. Marks. 1998. "Does Professional Community Affect the Classroom? Teachers' Work and Student Experiences in Restructuring Schools." *American Journal of Education* 106 (4): 532–75.

McLaughlin, Milbrey Wallin, and Joan E. Talbert. 2006. *Building School-Based Teacher Learning Communities: Professional Strategies to Improve Student Achievement*. New York: Teachers College Press.

Noe, Raymond A. 1986. Trainee Attributes and Attitudes: Neglected Influences on Training Effectiveness. *Academy of Management Review* 11 (4): 736–49.

Pang, Nicholas Sun-Keung, and Ting Wang. 2016. "Professional Learning Communities: Research and Practices across Six Educational Systems in the Asia-Pacific Region." *Asia Pacific Journal of Education* 36 (2): 193–201. https://doi.org/10.1080/02188791.2016.1148848.

Prosser, Jon. 1999. "The Evolution of School Culture." In *School Culture*, edited by Jon Prosser, 1–14. Thousand Oaks, CA: SAGE.

Schoen, La Tefy, and Charles Teddlie. 2008. "A New Model of School Culture: A Response to a Call for Conceptual Clarity." *School Effectiveness and School Improvement* 19 (2): 129–53.

Stoll, Louise, and Karen Seashore Louis. 2007. "Professional Learning Communities: Elaborating New Approaches." In *Professional Learning Communities: Divergence, Depth and Dilemmas*, edited by Louise Stoll and Karen Seashore Louis, 1–14. New York: Open University Press.

Timperley, Helen, Aaron Wilson, Heather Barrar, and Irene Fung. 2007. *Teacher Professional Learning and Development: Best Evidence Synthesis Iteration*. Wellington, New Zealand: Ministry of Education. https://www.oecd.org/education/school/48727127.pdf.

Tziner, Aharon., Robert R. Haccoun, and Avi Kadish. 1991. "Personal and Situational Characteristics Influencing the Effectiveness of Transfer of Training Improvement Strategies." *Journal of Occupational Psychology* 64 (2): 167–77.

Vescio, Vicki, Dorene Ross, and Alyson Adams. 2008. "A Review of Research on the Impact of Professional Learning Communities on Teaching Practice and Student Learning." *Teaching and Teacher Education* 24 (1): 80–91.

Wenger, Etienne. 1998. "Communities of Practice: Learning as a Social System." *The Systems Thinker* 9 (5): 1–5. https://thesystemsthinker.com/wp-content/uploads/pdfs/090501pk.pdf.

Yamin-Ali, Jennifer. 2021. *Teacher Educator Experiences and Professional Development: Perspectives from the Caribbean*. New York: Palgrave Macmillan.

Zaky, Eman Ahmed. 2015. "Nature, Nurture and Human Behavior: An Endless Debate." *Journal of Child and Adolescent Behavior* 3:e107. https://doi.org/10.4172/2375-4494-1000e107.

4. Challenges to Sustaining Effective Practice Post Professional Learning

Introduction

Preparing teachers to face the reality of their classrooms is a challenge for teacher education programmes. Understanding learners and their learning needs could be a nemesis facing some teachers post professional learning. Feiman-Nemser (2001) underlines some factors that are, indeed, challenges to sustaining or even developing effective practice. Some of these are: connecting students and subject matter in age-appropriate and meaningful ways; students' language and culture and how they make sense of their physical and social worlds; students' racial, cultural, and socio-economic backgrounds differ markedly from teachers'; prospective teachers' own biases and personal experiences with diversity. She also identifies "the need for teachers to cultivate the tools and dispositions to learn about students, their families, and communities and to build on this knowledge in teaching and learning" (Feiman-Nemser 2001, 1018).

Cultivating new tools and building on contextual knowledge are critical to an approach to sustainability that values learning from experience with the change brought about by efforts to improve, combined with an ongoing effort to grow in the knowledge, skills and understanding of what the change is about (Katz, Earl and Ben Jaafar 2009). This aligns with the notion that students' needs should drive decisions regarding educator preparation, effective curricula and assessments, and resource policy, as we strive to remove barriers to school success (Darling-Hammond et al. 2020).

Also, as noted in our introductory chapter, major contributors to sustainability are the teacher preparation programme itself and the practice context. These are also two elements that interact with others to create a context that can facilitate or hinder the transfer of learning as depicted in figure 1 in chapter 1. Hence, a teacher preparation programme that does not reflect an understanding of teachers' practice context cannot contribute to effective practice that is sustainable. Further to this, a lack of understanding of how school culture is composed (Schoen and Teddlie 2008) and of the notion that the meaning of culture is linked to context (Prosser 1999) could lead to debilitated efforts to support teachers' effective practice.

> **CASE: EDUCATIONAL ADMINISTRATION**
>
> The factors that inhibit the application of theories and principles learnt in the DipEd were classified as systemic factors, school factors, student factors and educational division factors. Further expositions on this follow.

Systemic Factors

The term "systemic factors" refers to the education system in Trinidad and Tobago, which is led by the Ministry of Education (MoE) and which governs education policy and practice. Graduates indicated two ways in which the system worked against them that inhibited them from using the theories and principles that they learned in the DipEd programme in their schools. First, the graduates stated that even though they had undergone a professional learning programme in educational administration, they were not placed into formal leadership positions at their schools for a very long time after completing the programme, which limited the extent to which they could practise their leadership skills. Alicia spoke about a "feeling of not being accepted, not being allowed to practise in a formal way, both by the school and the educational division", meaning that although she had been trained in educational leadership, she had not gotten the position of head of department (HoD). Cassian stated, "I am not considered a 'leader' in administration because I am neither a dean nor HoD. But I will be acting HoD (science) in a few months when the principal retires. I consider myself a leader, though, because of my experience in teaching and knowledge and skills gained during my postgraduate studies."

Second, the graduates' comments indicated some regret about not being formally placed in leadership positions, and this can lead to apathy. Nevertheless, these graduates, as mentioned before, found ways to use some of the leadership skills learned in the DipEd programme at their schools. For example, they conducted clinical supervision workshops and mentorship programmes.

School Factors

There were a variety of school factors that participants felt inhibited them from applying the theories and principles learnt in DipEd. First, Alicia lamented that "there are no programmes in the school to encourage teachers to be independent...lack of recognition and reward for work done". She felt that having done action research in the DipEd programme, she was interested in doing more of this type of research, which she felt led to key insights into improving teaching and learning. However, she stated that within her school's context, action research was not encouraged. She also stated: "In my school there is no access to literature and data encouraging more action research in the classroom." She was the only participant who spoke about research in this way.

Resources

Participants referred to a lack of infrastructure as an inhibiting factor. They identified physical infrastructure and technological infrastructure. In terms of physical infrastructure, Bernadine stated that "the classrooms were not conducive...we do not have cupboards to keep stuff...we don't have language labs, and the furniture doesn't allow you to let students move around much". Cassian also referred to a lack of sufficient science labs in the school, which inhibited teachers from taking "lower-form" students to the lab since the space was reserved for use by the upper-form students.

In terms of technological infrastructure, Cassian stated that the internet was not available to students at school. She also indicated that there was a "lack of infrastructure in some areas to facilitate easy use of technology". Alicia shared that her school "didn't keep up with modern technological equipment and software that teachers could use in their classrooms to make learning more fun". She felt this inhibited having inclusive classrooms and catering to the diversity of the student population and their needs, saying "we only reach some of the students...there are a number of students that we don't reach because of the strategies we use...they are all traditional and there is software that can be used to reach these students and help them learn, but even if we put in a requisition for these software and equipment, like we need more projectors, we don't get them."

School Policy

School policy is a factor which one graduate identified as inhibiting the transfer of theories and principles learned in the DipEd programme into her practice. One such policy which Cassian identified as inhibitory prevented "the lower school" from having access to the science labs, "because priority is given to upper school".

Student Factors

Bernadine spoke to a culture where students want to be "told" what to do and not to have to think independently and take ownership for their learning. She explained

> ...one of the things too is that our students are still in the mould of being told what to do, and that's one of the challenges that I face because, as I said, I keep trying to tell them 'Take responsibility for your own learning, understand, ask yourself why am I doing this, this is the objective, you know' and so that's one of the problems I think we face, especially in a traditional school like this.

Cassian also referred to a student culture that inhibits the application of theories and principles learnt in the DipEd, she referred to "students' reluctance to engage in activities that take away from their 'note-taking' time, because at the end of the class they think that 'copious amounts of notes' is an indication that learning took place".

Discussion

These graduates' experiences show that despite their own inclinations to improve their practice and their students' learning, there are contextual and cultural factors at their schools and in the wider system which provide roadblocks that inhibit them from doing so. The wider system, which Prosser (1999) refers to as the "wider culture", seems to have negatively impacted these graduates and in so doing, highlighted the "generic culture", which Prosser also speaks about, since similarities exist among the schools. While they had expectations of having their professional learning formally recognized through promotion, their expectations collided with the way in which national policy provides for promoting school staff. At the national level, the MoE and the Teaching Service

Commission, which are the bodies responsible for promoting school staff, have a rather bureaucratic promotion process. This process involves identifying vacant leadership positions (which may not exist at a graduate's current school), advertising the position, interviewing candidates for the position and then appointing someone to the position. The process is lengthy, and there is a sense in which the graduates perhaps should know this and therefore not have expectations to be upgraded too quickly.

Nevertheless, the "organizational structure" and "quality of the learning environment" (Schoen and Teddlie 2008) impacted negatively on the graduates. For example, in terms of the former, the graduates felt that the school did not recognize them as "leaders", this despite the leadership activities in which they engaged the school staff (clinical supervision and mentoring), which would potentially improve the "quality of the learning environment".

REFLECTION

One would think that graduates would be encouraged at all costs to implement the theories and principles that they learned on a programme of professional learning, especially when such implementation can engender school improvement. However, these graduates' responses show that this is not a given, that circumstances and conditions within the school environment can and do inhibit education practitioners from improving their practice in their schools, and as a corollary their students' learning, even if they are motivated and have the will to do so. It is also interesting to note that students have been acculturated to the use of teacher-centred teaching strategies, which do not promote the thinking and creativity skills that they will require for the future that they have to live in. This, coupled with limited use of technology, certainly has the dangerous implication of schools not preparing students for the world in which they will have to live, but preparing them for a life in the past.

> **Questions to Discuss – Educational Administration**
>
> 1. In your experience, how has your school inhibited you from using theories and principles that you learned on a professional learning programme?
> 2. How were you able to mitigate the inhibitory factors you mentioned in one above?
> 3. What advice would you give to school leaders in creating opportunities for graduates of professional learning courses to practise what they have learned in those courses in their school contexts?

> **CASE: FOREIGN LANGUAGE**
>
> In this section, the factors highlighted by the four teachers were either systemic at the school level or student related. It is noteworthy that Dana, more than the other three teachers, articulated many details that she saw as hindering her effective practice in her school.

Systemic: School Level

Technology

In the case of Anthony, who said, "I'd love to use technology more", frequent use is stymied due to practical problems, such as lack of equipment or "malfunctioning equipment", and even unreliable Wi-Fi: "We have Internet that kicks in and out. It works off and on but in terms of the technology-rich environment that we want… to have, I think we're losing in that…But it was a mantra one year to focus on technology in the classroom, and we had things going for us but then I guess with things…wear and tear of any equipment…upkeep…I have that challenge." For this progressive teacher, this was evidently a setback in his quest for learner-centred teaching.

Dana was constrained by a litany of technological setbacks. "Lack of a computer room [and] language lab"; "lots of times the outlets aren't working"; "there's a lot of electricity shortages here"; she has "to borrow [the] TV and CD player from the Tech Voc [Technical Vocational] department"; "the internet is always down"; "most students don't have internet at home"; "if anything goes wrong with the laptop, the students can't afford to fix it. They bring it to school, and it stays there for a long time." She described her hindrances further: "If we had a properly modern equipped, computer-equipped language lab... that would certainly help because we have to tote around a big, massive radio...Yeh. You know? And a lot of times the outlets aren't working...because there's a lot of electricity shortages here." Furthermore, she explained: "I find I have to use a lot of pictures, the visual helps, but we have difficulties with that because we've only one computer lab and a TechEd lab, and most of them are being used most of the time, so I can hardly use it, so I have to...I make my own posters and stuff when I can." While Dana can be lauded for her efforts to make her own visual supports for her lessons, one can recognize the weight of the effort to deliver student-centred lessons in an environment that barely supports the use of technological resources in a digital age.

Brenda describes the barrier to using authentic language input for listening practice because of technological problems: "I just read for them"; "Some sockets don't work...sometimes the whole radio gone missing...and so I just don't bother...no electricity. No this, no that...."

The outpourings from Brenda and Dana seem to unveil a sense of frustration that risks disabling their will to implement what they learned about effective practice in the DipEd programme.

Resources

Dana's capacity to teach effectively was severely challenged in that, apart from having virtually no access to technology in the classroom, "the (photocopy) machines are often down", "students haven't all gotten textbooks...I don't rely on the textbook, almost never." "[Students] don't have notebooks, pens, pencils." The frustration in the teacher's description of her practice was quite apparent, especially when there were additional seemingly insurmountable challenges to face. While at the time of this research, the Trinidadian government provided all students in the first year of high school with a laptop, Dana explained that when the students' laptops malfunctioned, they were not repaired in a timely manner.

Brenda bemoaned the lack of access to facilities and human resources: "If we had a nice room where we can use and people had access to that room, that would be so good…you know… everything working and a technician." She is referring to the use of a room, it seems, because access to technology in each classroom was perhaps too much to hope for.

School-based Practices

Apart from the technological hindrance to his practice, Anthony reported that because of the school's overuse of portfolio as assessment, which overwhelmed students, he had to eliminate it from the foreign language assessment practice. This, he felt, hampered the department's efforts to use alternative assessment. It would seem that some assessment coordination was needed school-wide.

Celia's school's workload policy negatively affects the time she could use to plan lessons. She describes the average workload as "extremely demanding, beyond the actual teaching" (cafeteria supervision an hour, once a week); demands on form teachers; writing lots of reports; "sometimes you feel like you're wasting time putting things on paper". In this case, workload extended beyond classroom preparation and teaching.

When Dana acted as HoD, reports from clinical supervision which she conducted "just remained in a file there and who knows where they are now", compounding her frustration with the system. The school appeared to lack a system for supervision of teaching, which includes follow-up.

Although Brenda seemed willing and had the drive to support the students at her school, as she did with the graduation celebration, the system of decision-making in certain areas did not allow her to contribute as she would have liked to. When it came to curriculum, exams, timetable and such things, she said, "there's a little oligarchy...who is involved in that...And so with me, with my new fresh ideas, they will not survive in that group. We do the same old things." While she prefers not to accept the "old things", she does so out of resignation.

Uncooperative Department

Unwilling colleagues curtailed the zeal of the recent graduates of the programme, as in the cases of Brenda and Dana. Both had acted briefly as HoD, and each had had unsatisfactory experiences. Brenda had initially attempted to host small workshops for her department when she acted as HoD:

> I used to do it in the past...I got discouraged...In the past, ...when I had now come out fresh from DipEd...I had little staff meetings. At that time, I assumed acting HoD...and I had little staff meetings for the group...to show them my lesson plans and what we could do and discussions...But two of the teachers, they were not receptive...because as far as they were concerned, these children and these children and what and what. They were young teachers. That was the sad part of it...They just discouraged me...they didn't even come to the meetings.

Dana acted as HoD for a short while. She reports her experience of the other teachers' lack of cooperation:

> Well, it was really interesting for me, but...I don't think the other teachers appreciated it very much...'Cause you see, there's a thing where...I have noticed, because we are more or less around the same age, I don't think they took it well that I would sit in on their class and that sort of thing...most of them the classes weren't structured...even though I went through the format that I used when I did DipEd, right? And...some of them they tried to do it...but it didn't always turn out so well.

> I think the main problem was when I offered suggestions and stuff, that didn't go down too well, so eventually I stopped.

While both Brenda and Dana would have had some knowledge and expertise to share, they needed some form of systemic school support to make a meaningful and sustainable contribution within their departments.

Student-related Factors

Student Culture and Behaviour

It was in the schools of Brenda and Dana that the factors hindering effective practice resided in either student behaviour or student culture. Dana says that "behaviour is always a problem". She recounted the incident of "a boy who threatened to kill me once, and I had to go to the police".

Brenda cited student culture and their view of school as a challenge to sustaining effective practice.

> Student culture – I think one of the barriers is that in this school they don't have no (sic) culture of study…no homework…I just come to a point where I just give up…because it makes no sense. No matter how good a teacher I am, at some point the learner must sit down and study too…Our children don't see the value of education…school is just…a holding bay…this is not really a learning institute for them.

As with Dana, frustration and the lack of will to sustain effective practice were somewhat evident in Brenda's sentiments.

Student Learning Ability and Socio-economic Background

Dana described her student population as follows: "Literacy challenges, learning disabilities" and "can't write properly, poor motor skills…more than half of the intake (of a class) is remedial." Based on this, Dana, as already indicated, found that "the DipEd programme…is more for an average to ideal situation". Added to the learning challenges she faced, she reported that many of the students were from "very disadvantaged homes, a lot of them work after school...a depressed community". Brenda shared that in her school "some children have severe social problems" and "disabilities". The latter is taken to mean learning disabilities. For these two teachers, these challenges posed a constant uphill battle.

Discussion

Organizational structure primarily, and quality of the learning environment, as well as student-centred focus were the dimensions of school culture (Schoen and Teddlie 2008) which had a negative impact on the ability to sustain effective practice to varying degrees among the four foreign language teachers. A "generic culture" (Prosser 1999) in both government schools was identified in the lack of technology and lack of access to the internet, although, while not pervasive, there was some element of this hindrance in one denominational school. But it was the overall lack of school-based systemic practices, such as an uncooperative department or lack of follow-up after clinical supervision, that hindered effective practice. It is not far-fetched to consider these elements as "the subterranean aspect of school culture", which refers to the micro-politics of organizations (Prosser 1999).

Interestingly, organizational structure impeded effective practice in one denominational school in terms of extra-curricular demands placed on teachers, and in the other case, the quality of the learning environment forced one teacher to deviate from best practice because teachers were overusing one particular type of alternative assessment. This hindrance highlighted, though, the teacher's attention to student-focused planning.

Student culture and behaviour, and student learning ability and socio-economic background were generic to the two government schools and hindered the teachers' effective practice there. The negative experiences of those two teachers with the hindrances that seemed insurmountable can be the result of their response to the impact of the "wider culture" (Prosser 1999) at their schools. We are reminded of the comment of one: "The DipEd programme...is more for an average to ideal situation."

REFLECTION

The challenges of sustaining effective practice post DipEd varied among the four teachers. All the challenges that surfaced arguably appeared to be outside of the control of the teacher but were not pervasive. Some, such as availability of technology, workload, choice of assessment and departmental functioning, to a large extent, fall within the control of the school's administration. Brenda did not feel that the programme prepared her to deal with the learning challenges, weak school culture and low socio-economic factors which she faced. This points to a need for continuing professional learning for teachers as well as whole school interventions to deal with these challenges.

Questions to Discuss – Foreign Language

1. What are some ways in which the school's administration could help these teachers overcome the challenges they face?
2. What elements of school culture have these teachers identified in their discussion of challenges to effective practice, and how do they compare or contrast with the cultural aspects in your own teaching situation?
3. How could the DipEd programme have helped Dana with her challenges?

> **CASE: SCIENCE**
>
> The participating teachers mentioned some barriers which inhibited the use of the principles and theories to which they were exposed. Some of these barriers were classified as school-related factors, student factors, teacher factors, programme factors and external factors. In addition, time for tasks was mentioned as a key factor that worked against applying the principles and theories in terms of the teachers' responsibilities of the job beyond classroom teaching. Time required to address student misconceptions and time required for students of varying abilities were also factors. The categories of barriers are presented with excerpts from participants' interviews, which provide evidence of barriers induced.

School-related Factors
School Philosophy/Policies

School procedures and rules can also serve as barriers to teachers' efforts to adopt some practices to which they were exposed and can frustrate their efforts. For example, rules regarding the production or photocopying of material, the use of the school compound or the use of technology.

Mahalia indicated that "the office has a system where you have to give three days in advance [for photocopying]. This is theory but not in the *real* world."

Wilhelminah felt frustrated by what she thought were her good intentions to help students but which were interpreted negatively by school administrators.

> You have to go on the graph and see where they fall, and I am using that as a service and the Ministry is taking that assessment and seeing if the child needs further assessment. So, whether you are doing it here or out there, you are still doing it. And there are plenty children in here who need it. I am seeing it as helping the child, but they are seeing it as you are doing business on the compound. ...But testing would

> help a child a lot, even though other countries may not be using it, it's a good assessment for us in Trinidad here...Poor people (sic) children can't afford that. You know sometimes you want to be very very rigid with your rules.

Teachers are exposed to technology integration, but school rules can stymie their enthusiasm in trying these strategies or cause them to revert to traditional practices. For example, with respect to the school's ICT policy, Wilhelminah mentioned that lower-secondary students are not allowed to use their own ICT devices, and therefore "I have to copy it for the lower school." Teachers also become disenchanted when the policies at the level of the school do not match the theories to which they were exposed in the DipEd programme and which require behaviours that do not align with their new philosophy of education. In relation to streaming of students, Peter referred to the internal conflict experienced when school philosophy and policies do not align with his beliefs. He said:

> Okay, your environment and the biggest factor in the environment is the administrator and the people at the level of the Ministry of Education or the Division of Education. There is a lot of how to say dichotomy between practice and theory as far as education is concerned. Under no circumstances do I believe in streaming. Yet the first thing we have is streaming at the institution level and then within the institution we have streaming again. You have prestige and the less privileged schools...So why don't we practice what we preach? That dichotomy now puts one under tremendous pressure, because if you don't believe in the philosophy of diversity and inclusion, I could need...the resources that I am looking at will not be the ones that you see as essential. I could be begging from now until...and if the Ministry of Education and the administrator will not provide....

Wilhelminah lamented that the level of productive noise associated with certain student-centred strategies would disturb other teachers and that her school's policy of professional courtesy demands that all teachers not be disturbed in their efforts to teach the curriculum. She states, "MI [Multiple

Intelligences] requires we bring in song and dance.... where the classroom is situated, you can't disturb the other classes."

School policies in relation to assessment constrain teachers' practice, according to Sophia who felt that contemporary approaches requiring more authentic assessment did not fit in with the school culture since "at the end of the day, the school requires that students are tested with pen and paper".

School Culture

Some teachers referred to differences in teachers' values and the resulting peer pressure as creating a culture characterized by peer pressure and resistance. For example, Wilhelminah narrated a scenario in which her professionalism was challenged by a colleague and attempts were made to influence her practice negatively. The colleague consistently asked: "Why do you need to do so much (sic) labs?" Sophia referenced the challenges encountered as she worked with untrained teachers in her capacity as acting HoD, when negative responses to her suggestions caused her to experience some doubt and reticence: "I see it happening. After a while, they feel they are experts, even though they might not have done DipEd. And now that I am acting HoD, I would go to see them do a lesson...acting puts me in a position as well, where you have to bat in your crease."

School Resources

In addition to school culture/policies, school resources also contributed to the sustainability of practices to which they were exposed in the DipEd. The absence of support (human or material) hindered attempts to promote learning in the manner presented in the DipEd programme. For example, with respect to practical work, when the lab technician was not available to provide technical support. The lack of technical support also occurred regarding the use of ICTs, as well as the absence of secretarial support. While these were obstacles, the four teachers consistently found ways to circumvent these challenges, to obtain the resources, to provide the experiences suggested in the DipEd programme and hence to aid learning. Wilhelminah, Sophia, Mahalia and Peter illustrate. Wilhelminah said: "And I have no lab support. You could imagine when we are doing titration? If you have a computer, they have pictures, page by page, but not every time you will get a projector."

Sophia said: "We have a portable, if it's multi-media that needs to be set up, you have to look for the technician, and sometimes he isn't there as there are so many things happening …the lack of actually having one here [multi-media equipment in the lab] sets you back to show video, etc.."

In terms of the laboratory technician, she explained: "There are a lot of questions as to what is his job [specification]. Sometimes you tell him 'Tomorrow I am doing a lab' and then tomorrow comes, and he would not be there, so that of itself gives me additional work."

Mahalia expressed a similar view: "A simple thing that you want to give them a handout, a cartoon or something that you can use as a set induction, you go to the office and the photocopying machine break (sic) down."

Peter also referred to lack of resources for practical work: "The thing about it with the science is that you may not be actually able to do the practical, but the child should be able to do activities even if it is from the textbook that will eventually give him a grasp of the concept."

Inadequate resources resulted in room allocation for science sessions that does not necessarily support the use of appropriate strategies. For example, other non-science subjects are assigned to the lab even when science is timetabled. Sophia states: "We have a lab, but Spanish uses the lab." While Sophia has a working laboratory that is assigned another discipline, Peter's principal indicated that due to the "challenges with the lab being termite ridden, the scheduling of labs is affected".

For three teachers, class size, space and traditional arrangement of furniture were referenced as inhibiting factors in implementing theories/principles related to student-centred learning. For example, if there is enough space for individual hands-on activities or group work, students are provided with the opportunities. Wilhelminah commented on the lack of space for individual laboratory work: "...and in science, they do their labs and I do demonstrations or they do it if we have the space". Sophia felt that the classroom arrangement does not facilitate grouping according to ability. She commented: "The way that the furniture is arranged even in the classroom, it is still crowded if you have too large a class and varying abilities." Mahalia supported Sophia's view, invoking the image of student-centred lessons as seen in films presented in the programme, versus the reality in Trinidad and Tobago classrooms: "You see how the class is arranged? Rows. I saw some on television and also for some of the lectures and they showing you films in which desks are arranged in groups in sections. Student-centred learning. My thinking is with a huge class and many classes in Trinidad are over twenty-five. Let us be real."

Time

Time was identified as a major issue that affected teachers' application of theories and principles to which they were exposed in the DipEd programme. Teachers revealed personal concerns regarding teacher responsibilities which require time for extracurricular activities and for preparation of practical work, as well as assessment of laboratory reports as part of the SBA system. They also referred to the time required for classroom preparation to cater to differing abilities; the amount of disciplinary content to be addressed; and issues related to the fast-paced society in which we operate. The mismatch between the time allocated to science in relation to time required for student-centred approaches, such as addressing students' misconceptions, was also a major issue. Further, teachers indicated that the number of public holidays, as well as time for staff meetings and other professional learning activities, encroached on contact time between teacher and students. These activities and events reduced the time available for completing the syllabus of work, which is quite extensive. One administrator indicated that teachers' leave entitlements (number of sick and casual days) can reduce the contact time with students and often leads to use of a transmission approach to content delivery. These themes are illustrated as follows.

Teachers' Responsibilities

According to Wilhelminah, the teacher's role is multidimensional, and there is only so much time in the day for planning and preparation. She mentioned that at her school "the teacher also has responsibilities for extracurricular activities". Sophia was sometimes overwhelmed by the responsibilities associated with science teaching, especially in terms of preparation for practical work: "Sometimes you know it's so much. You have lab books. You know. Go to the lab, prepare even if you want to do an activity. It calls for you to take time, go down to the lab, ensure that things are organized."

Time Allocation to Subject

Some of the student-centred strategies require time for execution and assessment, which is often not provided as required. As Wilhelminah noted: "MI [Multiple Intelligences] requires we bring in song and dance. But it isn't practical with one period assigned to the subject." Mahalia endorsed the view that the system seems to conspire against the use of these strategies. She indicated: "Remember, it's only singles [periods]. So even if you want to bring them up to the lab, by the time they come up and settle...."

Curriculum and Assessment

Mahalia commented that formal systems for assessment erode the time available for teaching and hence the use of strategies recommended. She stated: "Unfortunately, how we have mid-term and the term is so crunched...When you're crunched for time, because the CAPE syllabus is three modules...with the Forms 4, I have to cut down that [practical work]. Just confine it to when we have lab periods."

Wilhelminah endorsed Mahalia's views and also referred to new strategies for assessment introduced by the Caribbean Examinations Council (CXC), which require time for planning and which she feels reduce the time available for teaching the curriculum. She explained the problem as follows:

> You know that they changed, that CXC moderators are coming here now! So, that is another problem. I have to get time now and choose the children who will do the investigative lab. They actually write out the plan and I have to be with them at some extra time to actually carry out the lab. And that is out-of-class time, because I have to choose six of them. I don't know how we will do it. And they have no free periods. There isn't lunch time. I have extra class. So, I have to work with the six of them and then run it again.

Syllabus Coverage

The content and syllabus dominated teachers' thoughts and actions, and they focused the time available for covering the syllabus, even though they recognized that student understanding was compromised. Mahalia said: "To me, if you really focus on student-centredness, misconceptions take longer to be cleared up; and frankly we don't have the time to let them take to come to that understanding." Closely impacting on syllabus coverage was the number of public holidays which reduced contact time with students. As Wilhelminah lamented: "When I look at the calendar, we are missing so many periods. If you see how many Wednesdays and Fridays we have something. Remember what happened last week (spraying for Chikungunya) and then a holiday. Then we have a staff meeting. It's ridiculous.... Friday, we have staff development and then another Friday is TTUTA [Trinidad and Tobago Unified Teachers Association] development."

Student Factors

In addition to the school-related factors, student characteristics and dispositions constituted another factor that hindered the application of ideas introduced in the DipEd programme. Student factors are presented next. In some instances, the students rejected or did not respond positively when teachers tried to implement ideas learnt in the programme. Some students were concerned that these strategies did not sufficiently focus them on the final exams or in some instances, they became overly excited and were difficult to control. Sophia addressed the nature of the task and students' responses to alternative strategies:

> If you know like...for example, using...Gardner's' theory that we all have different intelligences. Sometimes in Form 1, I would say to students "go and research scientists and come and present information". I would say to them 'you could present in song, as a poem, you could do a play. I leave it up to you'. And you would have everybody come up and reading a poem or read the information. You would hardly have a group that comes in and say, well, let me do a little dance or sing something. To me students always take the easy route out. I have never come across in my entire teaching tenure here doing that activity in Form 1. I actually have to force them if it is to do a play or do something else. I don't know if they are not seeing it. Perhaps if they saw it in action, they could replicate, but they are probably so accustomed to doing things one way, they continue. I have tried in the past to get them to make up a song, but I think students tend to shy away a lot from that.

Mahalia alluded to the resistance from students in exam classes and the exuberance of boys:

> That's why I like the lower forms because you have room to do these things. But when you getting up now to exam time when you have the syllabus to cover...Because sometimes the students say, "Miss, exam. So they want...'leh we focus'... because it's boys I am dealing with, and that is the tension because them (sic) could get out of hand and rowdy very

quickly...I know when students [are] reluctant. I would tell them, okay... show them the connections."

Teacher Factors

As highlighted with the student factors, teachers' characteristics and concerns were factors that mitigated against the use of ideas introduced in the DipEd programme. These include their efficacy with selected strategies, their needs and preferences and the level of understanding of concepts introduced in the programme.

Teachers' lack of confidence to successfully effect learning by adopting student-centred strategies mitigated against the use of such strategies. Two teachers referred to issues that were categorized as relating to "self-efficacy". Mahalia recalled her feelings of incompetence in using models to illustrate the structure of the cell and the resulting unintended consequences for some students.

> I will never forget: it was on cells, and again I gave them models to do. [I told them] bring the marble, and it would represent the nucleus. When I had to give the assessment at the end of the lesson, it was to label the parts of the cell. I get marble for the nucleus. And I did not have anybody to blame but myself, because I did not really stress...we get caught up in the activity, and I did not really stress these things represent...we are using it to help us understand the parts of the cell. So as far as some of them were concerned, it wasn't a large percentage, but to me you really need to stress more. We got caught up in the activity, and in the last five minutes, we see there are misconceptions; and this is what I was talking about. You try to explain so much and end up confusing the students more.

Sophia also revealed a concern about self-efficacy in using student-centred strategies. She explained, "I would say, if I want to say one of the things we were taught is that every child has the ability to learn...That would be true, yes. But do we have the time or capability to ensure that it can happen? So, for the person that is slow, or the person that cannot read, or whose thinking process is probably not in line with what I expect, then how exactly do I deal with that?"

Peter adapted the lesson planning process according to his determined needs and preferences. Consequently, teachers' choices became obstacles to planning as introduced in the programme. He said, "I would tell you the truth. I don't really do detailed lesson plans. What I try to do is to pin down the objectives. Now I have the idea of the activities I could do, but the questions are the most important things. Because if after the activities the students cannot answer the questions, it means that I have not... so the questions, you have to get those right."

Some graduates indicated that they did not fully understand some concepts introduced in the programme, for example, the concept of "big ideas in science". Consequently, there is little influence on practice. As Mahalia stated: "The big idea for science, that is, content. To be honest, I really did not understand that big idea thing, you know. I mean I understand the concept of the unit, the big idea. I told you I tend to go off track, so in fact the big idea might actually hamper...."

Programmatic Issues

There were aspects of the programme that teachers felt were not relevant to their work, resulting in a mismatch between the DipEd programme content and their school realities. For example, unit plan templates were introduced in the programme. The school demanded schemes of work and daily forecasts. As such, the teachers felt that unit planning added another layer of paperwork. Wilhelminah and Mahalia raised this issue. Wilhelminah said: "I think the unit plan is a bit too much paperwork for the everyday running of the teacher, but the scheme of work, yes; lesson plan, yes. I don't know if you remember but as a secondary teacher, [it] is not just teaching. You might be a form teacher. We have other responsibilities: extra-curricular activities...."

Wilhelminah also mentioned that the programme does not cater to their lived experiences of varying student ability. She suggested as follows: "But I think for the DipEd programme, we need strategies for slow learners. I know that you focus on multiple intelligences, but if you could bring in some information of actual techniques that you could use with the whole class setting, that will be a plus in the programme."

External Factors

Teachers felt that the society is examination-oriented, with success measured in terms of the performance at national high-stakes tests (such as SEA) and regional examinations, CSEC and CAPE. They seem trapped in a web of conflicting values about the purpose of education – societal messages about examination and certification and the focus on meaningful learning that the DipEd encourages. Consequently, they are often caught up in the dilemma of either teaching to the test, using traditional strategies which seemed to have produced the desired results, or using contemporary approaches that are meant to enhance learning and meaningful understanding. Mahalia viewed the issue through a societal lens. She opined:

> I talking about society now. You telling me, you focusing on who comes first in SEA. Then scholarships. Oh, this school they get twenty something but if…so you telling me this is the cutting-edge way that you should teach, but to get these traditional results where it is…Lack of care in education system…So what tends to happen, yes, you would try to use the student-centred approach, but you know what, CXC and then CAPE, that's there, and sometimes you just fall back into "you have to learn this". I don't know if this is a cop-out….

Peter seemed to have buckled under the societal pressures: "I will locate the tutorial for them. Like even using like a photo story. I am trying to mix the traditional with the… but the problem is at the end of the day with CXC, you don't want to overwhelm them because you don't want to compromise the exam."

In addition to conflicting values on the purpose of education, on occasion, the MoE policy reflects old-fashioned values that militate against the adoption of ideas introduced in the DipEd programme, such as "Bring Your Own Device". Sophia recalls that "Ministry had actually sent out a policy that the use of cell phones was to be banned in schools...but the way the technology is going, you can't really say that...."

Discussion

The dimensions of Schoen and Teddlie's (2008) school culture that were most applicable to the factors hindering the sustainability of effective practice among the science graduates were "professional orientation", "organizational structure" and "student-centred focus". With respect to professional orientation, at one school, a teacher's subtle attempt to undermine the DipEd graduate's behaviours and to perhaps maintain the status quo reflected a lack of professionalism towards the graduate. The DipEd graduate had acted in accordance with the professional judgements concerning her students' needs, and her decisions were not respected. Besides peer pressure between colleagues, it was also evident that teachers' consistently negative attitudes towards another DipEd graduate, who was acting in the capacity of HoD, can also chip away at graduates' good intentions to improve the quality of the learning environment. Such behaviours reflect a lack of professionalism. These negative responses were also evidence of a negative micropolitical culture in operation at the workplace. Further evidence of the micropolitics at work in one school was teachers' resistance to clinical supervision. So strong was the resistance that "clinical supervision" was renamed "class visits", which can be interpreted as an attempt to flatten the organizational structure. The practices of undermining colleagues and superiors and the negative attitudes towards new approaches to teaching and learning described constitute a "generic culture" (Prosser 1999) that has emerged within both types of public schools. The outcome is contextual challenges in applying the theories and principles of effective practice introduced in the DipEd and maintenance of the status quo. Along with the negative generic culture within school contexts, influences from the wider culture (Prosser 1999) can prevent graduates from applying the principles and theories to which they are exposed. Examples included the society's obsession with examination and certification as well as policies emanating from governmental and regional agencies, and Mahalia's conceptualization of assessment as being different from pedagogy. In addition, the reasoning behind the absence of a "student-centred focus" at the lower-secondary level was unique to the case of a female teacher within an all-boys' school. Attending to gender-related learning demands and the boisterousness of younger male students can sometimes overwhelm female teachers, preventing the operationalization of a student-centred focus. Consequently, within a context where any one factor, or a confluence of factors, is manifested, sustained effective practice is hindered and the quality of learning and student achievement can be negatively impacted.

REFLECTION

Teacher professional learning can be conceptualized or theorized as a necessary input into reform of teachers' practice. That reform efforts are often unsuccessful or fall short of expectations can be linked to cultural and contextual factors within the school, which are deeply entrenched and difficult to change. Consequently, there is often an insignificant transfer of knowledge from the teaching context to the practice context. Often encountering societal values which support the status quo and which may send messages that conflict with the concepts and theories that advocate change or colleagues who are resistant to change, teachers can find that the role of change agent is unattainable. The resulting disappointment or frustration can lead to behaviours that create an adversarial relationship between, for example, student needs and the need for syllabus coverage, often with expectations for syllabus coverage exerting the more powerful influence. Faced with such cultural and contextual resistance, programmes such as the DipEd programme may then perhaps unfairly be deemed irrelevant to the teachers' everyday realities.

Questions to Discuss – Science

1. What model of professional teacher development would you promote to reduce the challenges described by science teachers?
2. How can teacher educators address the challenges described by science graduates?
3. Which, if any, of these challenges have you experienced as a science teacher and how did you address these challenges?

Conclusion

Based on our discussions and reflections on our findings regarding the challenges that DipEd graduates face in sustaining effective practice in their professional contexts, several perspectives shape our conclusion to the issue.

In all three specializations, there was evidence of how the dimensions of culture, as categorized by Schoen and Teddlie (2008), can impact each other. For example, organizational structure can be seen to limit the positive influence on the quality of the learning environment when graduates' input is absent, limiting the potential to apply principles and theories that they had been exposed to in the DipEd programme. Most either had to wait a long time to be placed in a formal leadership position, sometimes resulting in apathy, while others tried to use their skills and knowledge to mount learning opportunities for colleagues at their school. This link between how organizational structure can prove to be a barrier to quality of the learning environment and even to a student-centred focus was also evident in examples from the foreign language teachers' context where demands were placed on a teachers' time outside of class time, thus limiting time for teaching-related asks, and in another school where the choice of a student-centred assessment type had to be abandoned due to a lack of whole school assessment management. Quality learning was impacted negatively by the nature of practitioners' professional orientation, in some instances. For example, it was negatively impacted in the area of science where, possibly to maintain the status quo, one colleague undermined another's attempts to develop effective practice by resisting change in strategy of approach. Professional orientation was thus not devoid of micropolitical activity, which was present in both science and foreign language scenarios.

In addition to the interplay among the dimensions of school culture, as defined by Schoen and Teddlie (2008), the phenomenon of "wider culture" as described by Prosser (1999) appeared to impact the "generic culture" of certain schools, inhibiting graduates' ability to sustain effective practice as in the case of all three specializations. The "wider culture" negatively impacted graduates' practice across all three specializations. For example, promotion policies and a lack of recognition of leadership qualifications impacted educational administration graduates. Societal pressure negatively impacted science graduates regarding academic performance and certification, and policies emanating from governmental and regional agencies. Even in the midst of passion, vision and commitment, and school support, teachers' efforts can be stymied in a context where students, as in the science case, do not respond positively to new strategies to which they were introduced during a programme of professional learning. The 1992 study by Brickhouse and Bodner (quoted in Polman 2000, 124) found "…students' reactions to classes impose constraints on teachers' actions".

Foreign language graduates were negatively impacted by student values and attitudes, their learning ability and socio-economic background, which had consequences for the graduates' effective practice. This is reminiscent of Feiman-Nemser (2001).

While the hindrances to sustaining effective practice in the contexts presented in this study were not all pervasive, it would seem that the DipEd programme, which is for initial teacher preparation, is insufficient if we are to expect graduates to face the realities of their practice contexts and apply principles that will sustain quality teaching and learning. We are reminded that sustainability must be supported by new tools and attention to contextual knowledge when planning for change (Katz, Earl and Ben Jaafar 2009). As graduates make efforts to transfer their initial learning to their professional practice, any attempt to support this transfer, including through continuing professional learning, must factor in any cultural or contextual potential threats to sustainability. A suggestion is that the framework of Angelides and Ainscow (2000), could analyse "critical incidents" to gain a deeper understanding of school culture as it applies to preparing teachers to function effectively in their practice contexts.

References

Angelides, Panayiotis, and Mel Ainscow. 2000. "Making Sense of the Role of Culture in School Improvement." *School Effectiveness and School Improvement* 11 (2): 145–63.

Darling-Hammond, Linda, Lisa Flook, Channa Cook-Harvey, Brigid Barron, and David Osher. 2020. "Implications for Educational Practice of the Science of Learning and Development." *Applied Developmental Science* 24 (2): 97–140. https://doi.org/10.1080/10888691.2018.1537791.

Feiman-Nemser, Sharon. 2001. "From Preparation to Practice: Designing a Continuum to Strengthen and Sustain Teaching." *Teachers College Record* 103 (6): 1013–55.

Katz, Steven, Lorna M. Earl, and Sonia Ben Jaafar. 2009. *Building and Connecting Learning Communities: The Power of Networks for School Improvement*. Thousand Oaks, CA: Corwin Press.

Polman, Joseph L. 2000. *Designing Project-Based Science: Connecting Learners through Guided Inquiry*. New York: Teachers College Press.

Prosser, Jon. 1999. "The Evolution of School Culture Research. In *School Culture*, edited by Jon Prosser, 1–14. Thousand Oaks, CA: SAGE.

Schoen, La Tefy, and Charles Teddlie. 2008. "A New Model of School Culture: A Response to a Call for Conceptual Clarity." *School Effectiveness and School Improvement* 19 (2): 129–53.

5. Contribution to School Development and Beyond

Introduction

In their study of secondary schoolteachers in the Seychelles, de Comarmond, Abbiss and Lovett (2016, 95) saw "connectedness" as being relevant to teacher commitment. Their analysis of teachers' descriptions of teacher connectedness saw it to be a "sense of belonging to school", "professional responsibility", and "participation in school life". Evidence of such "connectedness" to school would be the "positive relationships that teachers developed in their schools and community" (99). They quote one teacher who viewed connected teachers as those "who are willing to promote teamwork in the school and community" (99). Further to this, the data from their study revealed that involvement in school life and school activities indicated teachers' sense of belonging to the school as their workplace.

For this "connectedness" to school to have an impact on school development would no doubt require that graduates of a professional learning programme, such as the DipEd, function as members of a community of practice as they seek to contribute to the development of their schools. An effective teacher education programme will prepare teachers to hone their skills in order to translate their philosophy of teaching into meaningful actions. However, a commitment to lifelong learning in its many forms (Burke 2002; Good, Biddle and Godson 1997) is essential to enable programme graduates to position themselves to recognize how they might contribute to building their school. In addition, the role of school leadership is critical in encouraging and supporting teachers through learning opportunities and organizational conditions conducive to sustainable effective teaching (Australia Victoria DET 2005). Moreover, we agree with Harris and Jones (2017, 2) who argue that: "... professional learning with impact is not an isolated or an isolating activity. Rather, that it is a collective endeavour where the idea of creating, building, and sustaining 'professional capital' is central. This 'professional capital' approach embodies teacher-led reform and advocates that teachers should take greater command of school and system improvement."

To bring about school improvement, educators must go beyond participating in professional learning programmes to use their new-found knowledge and skills to make contributions in their schools, communities, districts and systems. This is a kind of "visible learning" (Hattie 2012), which in essence is metacognition.

CASE: EDUCATIONAL ADMINISTRATION

The data showed participants contributed to the development of the school and the schools' communities in various ways. Additionally, Alicia showed that her contribution had moved beyond the school to other schools and the educational division. These contributions are discussed under five main subheadings below.

Programmes or Workshops Devised for School Development

All three participants had organized workshops for school development in varying measures. Alicia had devised clinical supervision workshops for HoDs at her school to develop their competence and skills in conducting clinical supervision with their teachers. She also organized a science exposition at her school. Bernadine had devised a "Form Teacher Programme" at the school to structure and guide the interaction of teachers and students. She had also developed an "Ethics Programme" for participation by non-Catholic students while their Catholic counterparts engaged in religious instruction. Additionally, she created the school's student handbook. Cassian, as mentioned earlier, had planned a professional learning workshop for teachers at the school on lifelong learning and making changes to facilitate teaching the twenty-first-century learner.

Influence on and Involvement in Decision-making and Policy at the School

The data indicated that there were both formal and informal influences on school policy. In terms of the latter, Alicia, for example, stated that she would be asked from time to time to sit in on HoDs' meetings, during which time policy would be discussed and decisions made. Cassian also felt that she influenced policy informally "when the principal asks her opinion". Bernadine was the one graduate who indicated that she formally influenced policy in her role as a member of the school's middle management team, responsible for making policy for the school. She gave timetabling and developing rules to govern student and teacher practices in the school as examples. Bernadine is also the person who registers students for the CAPE examinations, and in her role as registrar, she is involved in formulating policy to govern the registration process.

Involvement in Research That Has Impacted the School

All participants indicated they were involved in some form of research, either as part of a master's degree programme, in the case of Bernadine and Cassian or, as in the case of Alicia, doing literature reviews on, for example, clinical supervision. In all cases, the graduates' research impacted their schools. Bernadine had done a master of educational leadership and management and her research focused on ICT integration. She stated that her research focus was intentional: "I want to develop the use of ICT at school. It would make lessons more interesting for the students, so I felt I should gain the competence in this area." Cassian also mentioned that she had done a master of education, in which her research thesis focused on "developing a mentoring programme for a novice science teacher", who Cassian states is "now skilled and confident". Alicia did a comprehensive literature review on clinical supervision so that she would be better equipped to deliver the training workshops on clinical supervision that she did for her school.

Involvement in Committees and Groups at the School

All graduates contributed to their schools through their involvement in committees and groups in school. Alicia served on her school's Graduation Committee and chaired the school's Science Exposition Committee. Additionally, she stated that she would be asked to sit in on middle management meetings. Bernadine was a member of her school's middle management team, ethics committee and the committee to develop a curriculum for the "form teacher period". While Alicia and Bernadine's involvement in committees and groups was more at the administrative level of their schools, Cassian's was focused more directly at the student level and in particular at well-being and social and cultural issues. For example, she coordinated the following clubs: Zumba, aerobics, health and fitness. She also coordinated the school's parang group. Cassian justified her involvement in student-focused activities: "I get involved in extracurricular activities so that students see that learning can occur outside the classroom (even in non-academic settings), and I get to know them better and observe the skills that I would not normally see in the classroom."

External Stakeholder Relationships

All graduates in one way or another were engaged in activities to build external stakeholder relationships. Bernadine did this on three levels: parental, former teachers and corporate. In terms of relating at the parental level, she stated, "I interact with leaders of the Parents' Council to make decisions to improve the school and students." She connects with former teachers "to get advice on teaching issues, support for school projects, like giving of their time". At the corporate level, Bernadine interacts with businesses to get sponsorship and donations to fund projects in the school. Alicia's relationship and contribution with external stakeholders was more at the system and community level. She stated, "I've worked with the Division of Education to do workshops for teachers on how to prepare students for School Based Assessments." Alicia also works with other schools [she names the schools], primary and secondary in the area to guide them on conducting clinical supervision. She is also a CSEC moderator, and in this capacity, she moderates for School Based Assessments in the area of science.

Discussion

The graduates' contributions in their schools and wider communities reflect all four dimensions of the Schoen and Teddlie (2008) model of school culture. In terms of the "Professional Orientation", there seemed to be a desire and effort by the graduates to institute activities to ensure there was a high degree of professionalism among staff in their schools. This was done through activities such as mentorship programmes for novice teachers, workshops on how to conduct clinical supervision and how to prepare students for the SBA component of the CSEC examinations. The graduates were concerned with improving not only the level of professionalism in their own practice but also that of their departments and other departments within their school. Further, Alicia was concerned about raising the level of professionalism within her school community, by conducting professional learning to improve teachers' ability to deliver particular aspects of the science curriculum and conduct clinical supervision.

All these efforts of the graduates highlight the "Organizational Structure", which in this case shows that the style of leadership at the school was participatory, such that these graduates, though not holding official leadership positions, were allowed to demonstrate leadership by taking the initiative to find solutions to problems and implement these solutions to the benefit of staff, students, parents, community and division. The contributions of the graduates, through the programmes and activities they were involved in at their schools, were all devised to support student achievement, which aligns with Schoen and Teddlie's (2008) "Student-Centred Focus". It is significant that Cassian, for example, focused on using the psychomotor and affective domains to support the development of the whole child because these domains tend to be subjugated to the cognitive. The graduates' contributions also align with Schoen and Teddlie's (2008) "Quality of the Learning Environment" positively, by improving the quality of teaching and learning. On the one hand, they engaged in activities to improve teacher quality through mentorship programmes and clinical supervision. On the other hand, Bernadine and Cassian engaged in activities with students directly to improve their well-being and achievement.

The graduates all belonged to schools, each with its "unique culture" (Prosser 1999). Yet the contributions of these graduates also reflect Prosser's "generic culture", as there were similarities in the value the graduates placed on improving their schools, communities and students across the three schools. It is also reflected through the graduates' desire to seek continuing professional learning by engaging in further academic studies. The work of Alicia with other schools in her community and within her education division demonstrates what Prosser (1999) calls the "wider culture", which "emphasises the relationship between the national culture/s and that of the school, and recognises that the two impact and influence each other".

REFLECTION

Professional learning should have impact and should transform the participants and their practice in some meaningful way. These findings show the DipEd programme had an impact that precipitated transformation in the graduates' practice. There was impact in terms of their own school improvement, through the mentorship programmes, clinical supervision workshops, clubs, groups and committees which they were involved in. The work done by Cassian with her clubs and groups sought to improve the well-being of students, and this is something often overlooked in schools. The graduates' work sometimes impacted other schools, their communities, with the work they did with parents and the former teachers and also at the system level with the work Alicia did within her education division. This evidence is significant, because it means that the DipEd programme added value to these graduates, and they in turn added value to their schools and communities.

Questions to Discuss – Educational Administration

1. What are some ways in which you add value to your school and community?
2. What strategies can school leaders employ to ensure that staff who have done leadership preparation can contribute in such a capacity in their schools?
3. How can schools build their external stakeholder relationships?

> **CASE: FOREIGN LANGUAGE**
>
> The four teachers who participated in this research all made contributions to their schools' development. Apart from within their own classrooms, the teachers seemed most keen on making an impact in their subject areas. However, Dana's contribution to school outside of the classroom, as reported by herself and her HoD, was significantly lower than her three counterparts in this research.
>
> The ways in which these teachers contribute to school development fall within four broad themes: contribution to the Foreign Language Department, teaching resources, areas outside of foreign language, and active responses to school issues.

Contribution to Foreign Language Department

Anthony tried to influence his foreign language colleagues to use context in their teaching, something that was strongly emphasized in the foreign language component of the DipEd programme, since context is a major element of linguistic proficiency. A proficiency orientation to language teaching promotes communication in authentic contexts in the foreign language. As such, foreign language teachers are encouraged to embed all their lesson activities in a real-world context. Anthony also collaborates with his departmental colleagues: "It's always a collaborative effort, so whatever I'm doing in my classroom...I would share with the others." When foreign language was made compulsory in his school and he could not win the argument of encouraging the children to study it, rather than obligating them to do so, he used his influence. He said, "I started to encourage my colleagues to reorient their thoughts about how we deliver the curriculum for the first form." This was in an effort to motivate the students to do the foreign language at the examination level in Form 4. His HoD commented on the ease with which colleagues approach him for the mutual sharing of ideas.

Celia organizes co-curricular activities for her students, one of which is French breakfast prepared for the students. She explains the activity: "We have something called... 'the French breakfast' in Form 2, which is an informal assessment where the students have to be able to ask for the breakfast items and we actually provide the breakfast for them." The collaboration which began with her DipEd colleagues had now extended to a teachers' "Frenchbook" on Facebook, where she shares strategies. In terms of contribution to school, this enhances the quality of teaching and the reputation of the Foreign Language Department of the school.

We recall that Brenda had attempted staff development as soon as she completed the DipEd programme. She held departmental meetings and shared lesson planning and even did a demonstration lesson to help the other Spanish teachers in her department. Even though Brenda is not officially the HoD for foreign language, she unofficially coordinates the Spanish teachers according to the official HoD, who is actually an English teacher.

Though Dana offered no indication of how she contributes to school development, her HoD reported Dana had shown a keen interest in starting a sixth form Spanish class. Referring to the official post of HoD, her HoD added: "She kind of holds the Spanish Department together...but to say, to hold it, she would not be willing to do that." It would seem that it is the school context and the nature of colleagues that prevent Dana from assuming official responsibility at her school. We refer again to her earlier explanation: "I think the main problem was when I offered suggestions and stuff, that didn't go down too well, so eventually I stopped."

Teaching Resources

The development and use of effective teaching resources have the potential to influence how the student population and parents view the effectiveness of the school. In terms of creating and using resources to develop the quality of teaching and learning at the school, Anthony creates listening material for foreign language, using software. His HoD indicated that he uses online resources such as "Edmodo" to communicate with his students online, outside of school time. When Anthony recognized that using a commercial textbook did not suit the department's purpose of creating self-directed learners, he created a customized one for his school: "I decided that...if we want students to be self-directed learners...you must be able to give them opportunities for them to explore the material even before coming to class and not to wait on the teacher to say what is going to be done next. So that...those booklets were designed for first to fifth form over the six-year period so the student can work ahead." He also used data to inform teaching, especially regarding the use of the customized booklet: "We did surveys; we did a questionnaire for students...who did the exams last year." This type of initiative likely heightens both students' and parents' confidence in the school to cater to students' learning needs.

Celia, like Anthony, uses "Edmodo" to facilitate student work: "...and we've also recently started using Edmodo. Students are uploading their orals so that we don't have to necessarily go one by one. We post the questions or the reading passage, and they tape it and present it to us so we could listen to it and give feedback." Such an activity builds the reputation, which the school currently enjoys, regarding the adept use of technology in teaching.

No significant indications of contribution to school development via teaching resources were evident in the cases of Brenda and Dana.

Outside of the Foreign Language Classroom

Anthony has contributed significantly to areas outside of Foreign language: "I have also worked closely with the PTA (Parent

Teachers' Association)...for a number of years. I was the Welfare Officer and Education Officer of the PTA...to bridge that gap between what's happening in school and what the PTA here really wants to...so whatever their words are, they're aligned to what's happening in the school." He sees himself as having a role in school management through that involvement in the PTA. Having served at the highest executive level of the national Modern Language Association, he has planned professional learning workshops, which take him outside the sphere of his school. This teacher's contribution to development goes beyond his school. He has chosen further studies "because...I don't see myself just sitting in the classroom, as a basic classroom teacher. I really wanted to go out and...impact more on the students in [place named], so I wanted to see myself probably being a curriculum officer or something, where what I would do would impact more than just [my] high school students but...by extension, the [national] student population."

The HoD points out that he contributes to the school wherever he sees a need. Regarding an issue to do with male students in the school, she recalls: "I remember there was an incident...[he] was the one who picked up on it first, managed to do an investigation, counselled the boys and all of that before it got down to Admin...and out of the investigation, they agreed that ...he had done the right thing...because as ladies we never saw it. We never saw it, you know?" Further to this, the HoD signalled how he has made an impact outside of the school: "He received...Teacher of the Year [award], for [jurisdiction named] ...and out of that reputation...other schools and people with church groups and that kind of thing...he had to speak and make contributions to their group that way."

Celia contributes to school development through her attention to student discipline. She says, "I generally try to have good relationships with students, so you know along the corridor, even if I don't teach a student who's doing something wrong, I'm going to correct the student, ask the student his name, so build good relationships definitely so that...I find it pretty easy to correct the students...."

In addition, she focuses on student centredness by "building relationships with staff, students, you know, being involved in activities that the students would plan... and just trying to come up with creative ideas all the time to engage the students". Her HoD reported that Celia "likes to organize an etiquette session" for students and that "she's very much into subject selection. That's her forte." Both the principal and the HoD were able to corroborate her leading role in the development of the school's Benevolent Fund, which, as the HoD explained, "helps students, needy children who don't have books, who don't have money for transportation. She developed that fund."

As pointed out earlier, Brenda saw a need in her school to build the self-esteem of the graduating class. The students could not afford a graduation celebration as they would have wanted. "They wanted a more upscale [function]...to feel like everybody else." Therefore, she organized with other teachers to raise funds to facilitate the students' graduation for which the HoD indicates: "[Brenda] writes letters, for example, to get their [the community's] assistance and inform the people around about it." She contributes to the school culture by her involvement in non-academic activities: "I'm always involved in something ... and I get other people involved, too. Whether their heart is not in it, because it is me, they say, "OK. I will help...[whether] it is cultural, it is fund-raising, it is a drive for...to help a cause...." Her HoD verifies her contribution: "She's on the Divali programme, she does a lot, a lot. When we have teachers' retirement functions...sometimes she's in charge of different aspects of it and she handles it efficiently and professionally." We recall that Brenda did say she was "into school".

Dana's contribution to school development through student growth and exposure was confined to within school hours:

> I don't participate in extra-curricular much. When there is any activity, like any Carnival activity, or whatever, I would be

there with my class supporting that way. For example, every year...each class has to present a Carnival theme, around Carnival time. It's a Visual Arts project. So I definitely help my class with that. We get resources, have a presentation on that, so that's the way I would do it. But in terms of staying back after school and those things, I don't do those things anymore.

Active Response to School Issues

Contribution to school development went beyond activities teachers engaged in. Sometimes it required deliberate strategies to make a difference on the part of the teacher. Anthony "reflects on school matters outside of school time" because, as he says, "I always think that if I'm in an institution or any organization, I should be able to make an input." He continues: "So even sometimes we're on the phone up to midnight, just talking about what we observed in school today." He manages to make an input by bringing "the idea to administration because we cannot just work on our own programme. So we would have tabled the concern...at a meeting with the principal or vice-principal...even as a staff to know the nature of the issue so other teachers can now share their input, and they will see how we could devise a plan and get others on board to remedy – to address the situation."

The HoD confirms that Anthony voices his opinions in staff meetings. She also reported that he used his advanced studies to influence teachers' practice. He presents innovative approaches and colleagues get on board, as we have seen with his notion of "transactions". By acting on an issue, he has motivated students by approaching the issue from a student perspective. We recall his "Boys' Day" initiative, which was geared towards improving student behaviour and attitudes. Undergirding Anthony's approach to being a teacher at this school is the observation proffered by the HoD: "Tradition also plays a part because he would have come through the school and the people who taught us were also quality teachers...And so he has brought that and mixed it with what he has learnt... and so created a whole new product that we are trying to sell to other people now."

Like Anthony, Celia too was vocal on issues as she states: "Well, I am normally very vocal, so if I think there's an issue that needs to be addressed or I have a solution, a possible solution, I would normally go to [the vice principal or principal] or to my HoD." The principal verifies this when he says: "Well [Celia] is a very forceful contributor to discussions within the school. She contributes to anything in terms of the school development... she's always very interested; she always has pretty good ideas. And she clearly has the school's interest at heart."

She strengthens the school community by involving parents as well as the wider community: "I help our parent group and well now, we're actually planning a trip to Martinique...and we were thinking of once it gets established, we'd invite schools in the area to participate."

Influencing staff to get involved, expending effort in fundraising and logistics for retirement functions are ways in which Brenda contributes to school development. She describes her decision-making involvement as informal. Her modus operandi is "I just go to [the principal] and talk to her. I go with my idea; 'this is what I want to do'. I ask her if she approves, if she will go along." The HoD indicates that Brenda can contribute to the school's development in that she "would look at the discipline issues, try to talk with the deans, or the form managers...She would arrive at solutions through the deans, in consultation with them."

Discussion

It is evident that the contributions of these four foreign language teachers to their schools' development align with all four dimensions of school culture proposed by Schoen and Teddlie (2008). Their professional orientation, which translates into their teaching philosophy, was evident; but this combined with what they had learned in the DipEd programme, which were new strategies and the use of context that they felt compelled to share with colleagues. The organizational structure, through its leadership, facilitated and encouraged their involvement where it occurred, reflecting a student-centred focus. They were able to positively impact the quality of the learning environment through teaching resources that two of them created, which, apart from their own initiative, would have been stimulated by learnings and dispositions acquired in the DipEd programme.

What also emerged is the "generic culture" (Prosser 1999) of the schools where Anthony and Celia taught. What was common to them were the shared meanings (Schein 1992) which enabled them to integrate into their practice what worked for them in terms of a united effort to work towards their schools' vision. This may also be referred to as the "unique culture" (Prosser 1999), which facilitated the varied contributions of Anthony and Celia to a greater extent than Brenda and Dana. Perhaps it may also be said that the schools where Anthony and Celia worked had acquired a "perceived culture" (Prosser 1999), which attracted potential stakeholders like parents and potential students to those two schools which, to them, were the preferred choice for secondary education.

REFLECTION

Despite challenges they faced, these four teachers saw themselves as change agents in that they contributed to school development in several ways, which included acting upon their observations and analysis of matters, such as student discipline or student self-esteem. Attention to student development outside of the foreign language classroom was a priority for all four. In varying degrees, they seemed inspired and driven to build an effective school, with one of them being further motivated to make an even broader systemic impact.

Questions to Discuss – Foreign Language
1. In what ways does the school culture facilitate these teachers' contribution to school development?
2. How does the foreign language teachers' behaviour reflect a desire to build school culture and school climate?
3. Which of the teachers can you identify with in terms of contribution to school development and why?

CASE: SCIENCE
In most instances, for the four science teachers, school development meant the enhancement of the image of the school in the eyes of stakeholders and the public. This positive image of the school was achieved by improving student performance (through collaboration with colleagues, extra class activities, problem-solving related to teaching/learning, initiating culture change – new ways for curriculum delivery); contributing to a functioning management team; participating in committees to raise funds for school improvement; participating in activities that would promote the school as a first-choice school and assisting with developing systems to improve the efficiency of administrative functions.

Capacity Building
Collaboration with Other Teachers

The DipEd Science graduates narrated experiences that illustrated their willingness to share their expertise with less experienced colleagues. The four teachers provided examples of collaboration with colleagues and sometimes the HoD or principal corroborated these data. In some instances, the teachers shared their experiences of mentorship or instances where the teacher in the role of HoD provided the necessary leadership to junior teachers. The overall aim of engaging in these activities was to improve student performance. The following are examples of experiences of mentoring, collaborating with colleagues and sharing resources from the four teachers.

Wilhelminah reminisced on her interaction with a junior member of the Science Department. She said: "I sat with her, and we went through the scheme of work. It is senior teachers helping junior." The HoD corroborated. She indicated DipEd graduates mentor younger staff and that Wilhelminah is "dedicated and her results show it". Sophia reported a similar experience of collaboration within the Science Department, but this time in relation to resources and advice. She mentioned, "I 'shared resources' with colleagues." But Sophia also acted as HoD, and in the role she "gave advice to [the] Math Department".

Mahalia also shared resources with members of the Science Department. "If I make up a crossword, I will give it to the next teacher in Form 1. Or then he would be 'Okay, well I came across this.'" She said she was not hiding resources, as is the case in other schools. Physics and chemistry calculations were also shared.

Similarly, Peter indicated he shares ideas with colleagues within his department. However, he has advanced to another step of formalizing the collaboration by establishing a community of practice to address the issue of metacognition to improve student performance. He stated: "I am sure you are familiar with the concept of community of practice. A group of my colleagues and I are trying to use the notion of metacognition to improve student performance." Further, he elaborated on his actions to assist in professional learning of staff, as well as sharing his knowledge of and expertise in educational theories, thus: "I have another project that I am trying to design. The course in blended-learning in-house for our teachers here. Well, I am running that with one individual. But what I am discovering is that the biggest problem is time for most teachers. Right now, it is one of the IT teachers who has more time to deal with that." He added the following: "Okay, number one I try to share the knowledge that I have with my colleagues. I was talking about the knowledge of educational psychology and the knowledge of educational technology. In addition to that, where administrative duties are concerned, I try to help along with the implementation of technology."

Peter contributes to school development by enhancing administrative processes to address school needs more efficiently. His principal corroborated this, saying: "He computerized the reporting system which he introduced. His system was unique. It provided transcripts and teacher data."

In their attempts to optimize the strengths available in the department and improved student performance, two science teachers indicated that they had initiated changes that impacted the operations at the level of the department. For example, Wilhelminah initiated the model of team-teaching of chemistry at the sixth-form level. The new way of working required some negotiation with, and approval from, the principal, as indicated by the HoD. The latter said: "We have begun team-teaching at CAPE, which required some negotiation, but it is working." In a similar manner, Peter initiated the blended-learning model by developing a learning platform for online delivery by teachers at the school.

In sum, the teachers developed a collegial ethos within the department, which they felt would redound to the benefit of the students. They also indicated that they went beyond their duties during scheduled class sessions by devoting some of their free time for additional student-teacher interaction.

Student Development

Two of the four science teachers mentioned that they organized extra classes without remuneration, with the aim of improving student performance, which is linked to the reputation of the school. For example, Wilhelminah recalled that: "I used to give extra classes on an evening when I started. Now I do it in the lunch time and times I'm free. I have lunch time classes with them. It's a revision class, and it's mandatory." Sophia mentioned similarly that based on students' level of preparation, she felt the need for and arranged extra classes to address weaknesses. In addition to extra classes, teachers also initiated new processes within the department, which led to a culture change.

DipEd science graduates also contribute to school development by solving problems and addressing issues that can impact teaching and learning and consequently student academic performance. For example, they arrange for resources to facilitate individual or group work. Wilhelminah collects money to have copies of worksheets and activity sheets available when the school's machine is not functional and when policies seem to present obstacles to having copies made at school. Sophia ensures the availability of working resources to facilitate science teaching/learning. For example, she monitors resources such as the water still, which provides distilled water for practical work in chemistry.

The activities described above impact directly on the teaching/learning in the classroom. However, as illustrated below, the teachers also engaged in activities that impacted indirectly on student performance, such as their leadership role on the school's management committee, their interaction with external stakeholders and their use of research for strategic planning at the level of the school and lesson planning at the classroom level.

Leadership Roles

Two teachers contributed to school development by assuming leadership roles through their involvement in administration at the level of middle management. Sophia was directly involved in developing school plans as part of the executive management team. The principal corroborated the information that the teacher had provided. Sophia mentioned: "In my role as HoD, I sit in on the management meetings, and I helped to develop the school plan." Peter also acted as HoD and, therefore, was required to perform administrative functions. In so doing, he had developed technological solutions to manage administrative functions more efficiently. He explained: "In addition to that, where administrative duties are concerned, I try to help along with the implementation of technology to run the…It is kind of different now, because they have a different system, but those are my strengths."

Building Relationships with External Stakeholders

Three of the teachers' comments revealed their role in projecting a positive school image as they interacted with external stakeholders, such as the MoE, the public and with private and/or state enterprises within Trinidad and Tobago, which were aimed at enhancing the school's reputation.

Teachers also engaged in fundraising activities, for overall school development. The HoD cited Wilhelminah as a teacher on whom she could rely when the MoE requested lesson plan samples. She was able to respond positively to the MoE's request, which in turn characterized the school as an exemplar of good practice. She recalled: "Ministry sent for an example of an ICT-infused lesson, and as HoD, I was able to provide it from the files from Wilhelminah's class."

As mentioned previously, Wilhelminah assists with Open Day activities, which should promote the school to primary schools within the community as a first-choice school at the SEA examinations. Wihlelminah said: "As form teacher of Form 6s, I provided… [resources for] their displays and also assistance." Wilhelminah also contributes as a member of the fundraising committee and volunteers for the committee's "cookout." Funds raised at that activity usually provide financial support to students in need. Sophia is also a member of the Finance Committee at her school.

Peter also is involved in strategies to enhance the image of the school. He is a member of the branding committee, which meets for development of business ideas and to ensure quality.

Sophia responds to invitations from stakeholders for student participation in various competitions. For example, she supported students who entered a Water and Sewage Authority (WASA) competition.

Research That Has Impacted the School

Three teachers referred to the role of research in their practice. Wilhelminah's HoD referred to the role of research in strategic planning. Peter engages in a review of the literature on the concept of developing a learning community that focuses on metacognition as a strategy to improve student performance throughout the school. He said:

> Informal literature research regarding metacognition, for example. Let me tell you what is happening. I have an informal...I am sure you are familiar with the concept of community of practice. A group of my colleagues and I are trying to use the notion of metacognition to improve student performance. Not as I say from a big research. What I would go on the internet and do is to get articles, simplify the articles and pass it to them. We have a community set up. For example, just before Carnival two of my colleagues and I were talking about how we could get the students...and I was telling him about metacognition. So right now we have that going. It is not formal. I would give the class the information how much time they study, how much, but it is not to gather data in that way. Well, driven by informal research.

Mahalia referred to research for planning lessons and to being one step ahead of students:

> What I think is that DipEd...what has happened is once you get into that research mode, it never leaves you. So when you have to do research for an essay or you have to do research for the background of your curriculum study, you get into that mode. So that never left me. So I am preparing for this lesson, planning for planning and design lesson, them (sic) students asking, in a sense I am anticipating what questions they will ask me. ...So I think that is the thing, you must do research. That has never left me.

Wilhelminah's HoD, herself a DipEd graduate, mentioned: "We did a self-study in the process of developing our strategic plan. Based on questionnaires and data, decisions were made." But she did not refer to DipEd graduates' use of action research to address teaching/learning issues at the level of the class or at a departmental level.

Discussion

The analysis of teachers' contribution to school development revealed Schoen and Teddlie's (2008, 140) four dimensions of school culture in operation. Professional orientation was evident though initiation of culture change, as well as research for enhanced student learning. Teacher's involvement in management committees provided insights into the organizational structure and principal leadership as distributed. The teachers' disposition to solve problems to benefit the student science experience and learning pointed to their desire to improve the quality of the learning environment, and their collective efforts to support student achievement were evident in their efforts at collaboration. Student-focused development activities were evident.

REFLECTION

The four science teachers contribute to the development of their schools through their involvement in activities that go beyond teaching and learning actions in the classroom. It is likely that a desire to ensure a more efficiently functioning and highly regarded organization in the eyes of stakeholders underpinned their efforts at school improvement. So whether it is developing improvement plans, devising administrative solutions or ensuring resources for teaching and learning, it appears that these activities are considered important supports for teaching and learning within the classroom. Consequently, it appears that these science teachers have developed a professional identity that accommodates a multidimensional role of the teacher, which augurs well for school development.

It is of concern, however, that teacher-as-researcher, which can significantly support school improvement and which was a significant component of the DipEd Programme, is not a significant component of the science teachers' professional identity.

Questions to Discuss – Science

1. How do teacher education programmes address professional identity?
2. In what ways can teacher educators incorporate examples of science teachers' contributions to school development within the teacher education programme?
3. What is the role of action research in school development?

Conclusion

The goal of professional learning is to engender classroom and school improvement for the purpose of positively impacting student and staff learning (Hattie 2012; Jones 2021). Nevertheless, Harris and Jones (2017) warn that the effect of professional learning on its participants and by extension, the extent to which they transfer the learning from the learning context to their practice context dependens on the quality of leadership in the practice context. They state that "for teachers' professional learning to have the impact required or expected, it needs to be modelled, reinforced, and supported by those in formal leadership positions" (2). The Australian DET also comments on the role of leadership in creating a learning environment in schools that provides learning opportunities for staff (Australia Victoria DET). The synthesis across all three subject cases in this study confirms this view.

This chapter addressed how DipEd graduates contribute to their schools' development. All the graduates' experiences and activities post professional learning indicate they desired to see their schools as effective schools. This desire, coupled with the skills and knowledge gained from their professional learning, propelled them to be change agents in their school. The support and flexibility of the leadership at their schools facilitated their ability to enact change and make an impact through their contribution. Alicia, Bernadine and Cassian were allowed to use their leadership preparation skills to build capacity within their schools by implementing clinical supervision mentorship programmes for their schools. In Alicia's case, her impact was extended to the community and the educational district. The science and foreign language teachers also acted as change agents and with the support of their schools' leadership contributed to their schools' development in several ways, for example, building capacity within their departments by developing teaching resources and collaborating and sharing with other teachers. Some teachers also built relationships with external stakeholders, through the Parent-Teacher Association and activities, such as hosting Open Days for prospective incoming students. Had it not been for the alignment between the vision of the leadership in these schools and the initiative of the graduates to effect change, which was clearly born out of the "connectedness" (de Comarmond, Abbiss and Lovett 2016) that graduates felt to their schools, these activities that ultimately can affect student achievement would not have occurred.

Professional learning programmes with collaborative research and inquiry embedded have a greater impact on sustaining graduates' practice (Harris and Jones 2017). While some graduates indicated that since leaving the DipEd programme they had engaged in further studies at the master's level, for which they had to conduct research for their assessments, it is concerning that none has been involved in collaborative research at their schools, particularly as this is a significant component of the DipEd programme. However, conducting research at school takes time, and the graduates all seem to have heavy workloads. Thus, it could be a matter of prioritizing and not disinterest.

References

Australia. Victoria DET (Department of Education and Training). 2005. *Professional Learning in Effective Schools: The Seven Principles of Highly Effective Professional Learning*. Melbourne: Victoria Department of Education and Training. https://www.education .vic.gov.au/Documents/school/teachers/profdev/proflearningeffectivesch.pdf.

Burke, Gerald. 2002. "Financing Lifelong Learning for All: An International Perspective." Working Paper No. 46. Centre for the Economics of Education and Training (CEET), Monash University, Victoria, Australia.

de Comarmond Odile, Jane Abbiss, and Susan Lovett. 2016. "Commitment Crises: Voices of Secondary Teachers." In *Professional Learning in Education: Challenges for Teacher Educators, Teachers and Student Teachers*, edited by Bram de

Wever, Ruben Vanderlinde, Melissa Tuytens, and Antonia Aelterman, 87–111. Ghent, Belgium: Academia Press.

Good, Thomas L., Bruce J. Biddle, and Ivor F. Goodson. 1997. "The Study of Teaching: Modern and Emerging Conceptions." In *International Handbook of Teachers and Teaching*, edited by Bruce J. Biddle, Thomas L Good, and Ivor F. Goodson, 67–79. Dordrecht, The Netherlands: Springer.

Harris, Alma, and Michelle Jones. 2017. "Leading Professional Learning: Putting Teachers at the Centre." *School Leadership & Management* 37 (4): 331–33. https://doi.org/10.1080/13632434.2017.1343705.

Hattie, John. 2012. *Visible Learning for Teachers: Maximizing Impact on Teachers*. London: Routledge.

Jones, Ken. 2021. "'Professional Development' or 'Professional Learning' ... and Does It Matter?" Education Workforce Council. Accessed May 21, 2021. https://www.ewc.wales/site/index.php/en/about /staff-room/son-archive/43-english/about/staff-room/blog-archiv e/93-ken-jones-professional-development-or-professional-learning-and-does-it-matter.html.

Prosser, Jon. 1999. "The Evolution of School Culture Research." In *School Culture*, edited by Jon Prosser, 1–14. Thousand Oaks, CA: SAGE.

Schein, Edgar H. 1992. *Organizational Culture and Leadership*. 2nd ed. San Francisco, CA: Jossey-Bass.

Schoen, La Tefy, and Charles Teddlie. 2008. "A New Model of School Culture: A Response to a Call for Conceptual Clarity." *School Effectiveness and School Improvement* 19 (2): 129–53.

6. A Model for Sustaining Effective Practice

Introduction

This chapter presents key learnings from the findings on the status of graduates' practice, the factors facilitating and inhibiting the transfer of knowledge, skills and competencies developed within the learning context and transferred to their school context, as well as graduates' contribution to school development. It also presents a model, with evidence-based justifications, as a framework for sustaining effective practice. A key feature of the model for sustaining effective practice is the role of the context and culture of the institution in which the graduates engage in professional practice. We posit that graduates of the programme are within a liminal space where there is the potential for transformation. The implication is that the school context and culture must provide a supportive environment, which allows the seeds planted within the professional learning programmes to flourish. We, therefore, argue that context and culture matter in any attempt at professional learning that promotes sustainable effective practice as its goal. The following sections elaborate on the key learnings derived from the synthesis.

The Issue of Impact

A key understanding from this research that aligns with Hattie (2012) is that professional learning activities should have impact, and as such the programme itself should have a feature embedded within it to determine and measure such impact. It is insufficient for professional learning programmes to stop at the point of delivery and not consider the issue of impact. Delivery of a professional learning programme simply indicates that something has been initiated to improve the learning of educators, which it is hoped would improve their practice. Nevertheless, improvement in practice is determined by the impact of the programme on interrupting behaviours of educators within their contextual and cultural teaching and learning spaces. Still, it is the change in the behaviour of practitioners' post professional learning that creates an impact. This research has shown that to bring about impact takes time, sustained effort, collaboration, innovation, risk-taking and confidence. In particular, it requires an innate educational philosophy and belief that all students can learn. Further, it requires that educators have the efficacy to bring about such learning. What it therefore means is that the professional learning programme must be inspiring such that it empowers the participants to try different things and to use a variety of strategies and approaches to improve student learning. The DipEd programme displays these features, but sustaining the practices developed during the programme and strengthening the ideas introduced require a supportive school context and culture as teachers cannot do it alone. The liminal space in which graduates find themselves requires contexts that provide the appropriate facilitating factors so that transformation can be realized. Peter's attempts at developing a learning community to advance skills in ICT integration and Wilhelminah's initiative for team teaching, itself a collaborative venture requiring the support of the principal and middle management, are pointed examples. Additionally, Anthony's initiative of creating a booklet of teaching and learning materials shared by his department was facilitated by being given "room to expand possibilities". Similarly, Alicia provided training for heads of departments at her school on how to conduct clinical supervision. Additionally, she conducted workshops for teachers within her school and other schools within her district on how to do the School Based Assessment of the Caribbean Examination Council Examinations. These initiatives show that through her practice Alicia had impact within her school, as well as in her district context. Thus, it stands to reason that the level of autonomy and support that graduates have within their context (school and district) are important in order to promote and sustain their effective practice, post professional learning.

Smooth Sailing
Marriage of Personal Characteristics and School Environment

The marriage of a personal drive with exposure to the programme contributed to graduates engaging in and promoting activities to improve their schools. However, their contribution to school development depended on the extent to which the culture of the school allowed staff to be innovative and autonomous. Additionally, school culture largely relies on a leadership vision to grant students and educators the autonomy to take risks, learn from failure and be flexible to make changes as needed (Sheninger and Murray 2017).

Teacher autonomy was evident in the graduates from all specializations. Alicia in the educational administration specialization, for example, viewed herself as a leader in the school with a role in school improvement. She was able to fulfil this role because the culture in the school encouraged staff to share the skills and knowledge they acquired from professional learning. The culture of the school made Celia, a foreign language teacher, feel empowered to raise with middle management any issue that needed to be addressed and to offer a solution to fix it. Science teachers were driven to engage in problem-solving related to teaching and learning, initiated new ways of delivering the curriculum and even helped to develop administrative systems for more efficient functioning, all with the support of the school administration and other staff. These examples provide evidence that if the school culture is facilitative of effective practice, and graduates are intrinsically motivated, they can sustain and promote in their practice context what they learned in their professional learning programme.

The Rocky Road of Sustainability

The rocky road of sustainable educational practice is part of the landscape reminiscent of the notion of "teaching effectively in an imperfect world" (Hammerness et al. 2005), an imperfect world characterized by school culture and context, in addition to external factors such as the Ministry of Education and Teaching Service Commission policies that hinder the transfer of learning of programme graduates. If we were to consider effective teaching from a human development perspective, we might want to analyse its sustainability as Cilliers et al. (2020) did. Having evaluated the impact of two teacher professional learning programmes, they suggest that the cost-effectiveness of such programmes has to be measured more meticulously to include the impact of spillover to teachers in the schools who did not participate in the programme. They also suggest that more resources should be dedicated to better sustain initial gains from investments in human development. From a different perspective, providing support and educator preparation, well thought-out curricula and assessments, together with sound resource policy, all based on students' needs, can help to remove barriers to school success (Darling-Hammond et al. 2020).

Furthermore, the prominence society gives to certification puts pressure on teachers to conform with traditional practice, which is essentially "teaching to the test". One science teacher reported that students' negative responses to innovative strategies made her speculate about the appropriateness of a student-centred philosophy in her particular context. Another described the attempt to adopt new approaches as "an uphill battle" when it came to moving students forward in a new direction in her efforts to sustain effective practice. The hindrances to sustainability were also evident in teachers' inconsistency in using student-centred approaches. Frustration and roadblocks due to lack of supportive resources were cited as hurdles in the case of two foreign language teachers, evident of macro-systemic engine failure. For graduates of the educational administration specialization, sustaining effective leadership practice was complex, in that while they did not hold official leadership positions in their respective schools, they practised some of what they had learned from the professional learning programme. Still, the inability to practise some of what they had learned from the programme because they were not officially installed into leadership positions at their schools resulted in a roadblock for their sustainable practice.

A Model for Sustaining Graduates' Effective Practice Post Professional Learning

Description of the Model

The model presented is based on empirical evidence and our experience. It indicates how schools can operate to sustain graduates' practice post professional learning. The writers propose that there are seven main conditions that sustain graduates' practice at the school level. These are listed below, with deeper expositions on each and the role each plays in the model. Additionally, the writers believe that what is essential is continuous reflection, monitoring and evaluation of all the conditions and the educational practices within the school, to determine how they are working, if they are working and what might need to change to make them work. This is why the outer loop is included in the model. This model is being offered as an option and not as a prescription, meaning it may not be the only way forward, but it is certainly useful for key stakeholders whose experiences resonate with those described in this research, as well as for those who will be confronted with the realities of the education milieu. It provides a solid, and albeit comprehensive, global approach to sustaining graduates' practice within the school setting.

Deliberate and sustained effort and commitment to improvement is required, and as such it is an approach that must be intentionally led. The writers recommend a collaborative leadership team approach of internal and external education

Figure 6.1:   Model for Sustaining Graduates' Effective Practice Post Professional Learning

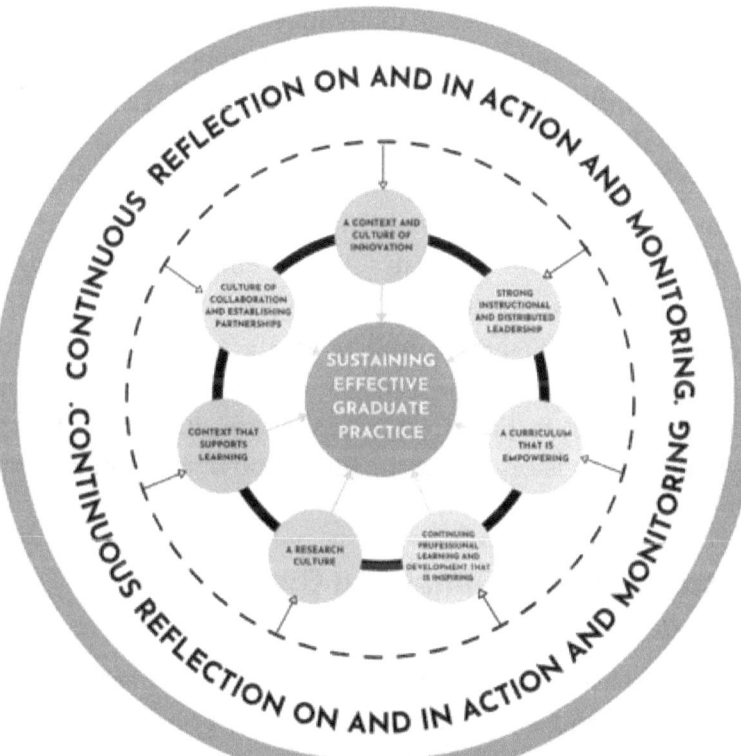

constituents. The team should be composed of, but not limited to senior and middle leaders at the internal school level, and externally, the university and state agencies connected to education. A beginning point in operationalizing this model might be forging the necessary partnerships among school, university and state to create the synergy which promotes continuous reflection on and in action and with monitoring. As a corollary, this collaboration can be an engine to drive policy that facilitates graduates' ability to effectively transfer knowledge from the professional learning space to the practice space. Elaborations of the conditions that sustain practice as presented in the model follow.

1. A Context and Culture of Innovation

The OECD (2017) describes an innovative learning environment as "fresh ways of meeting outstanding challenges in a spirit of openness to disciplined experimentation" (18). This organic definition allows for its application to different contexts. It also fits with the writers' philosophy that continuing professional learning is critical to schools being innovative and ensuring that the environment facilitates improvements and change. Such professional engagement may afford practitioners the opportunity to analyse and re-create as necessary their philosophy and how that is translated in the new vision of the school's community (Yamin-Ali 2014). With this model being presented, that vision would include innovative thinking by stakeholders.

2. Strong Instructional and Distributed Leadership

Instructional leadership is generally defined as the management of curriculum and instruction by the school principal. It is the type of leadership that drives learning in schools, both for teachers and for students. The role of the instructional leader is to be the key agent of change. In other words, the school leader is charged with the responsibility of creating an environment in which teachers can teach and students can learn. The writers suggest that to do so effectively, the school principal would need to employ distributed leadership since "at the core of the concept of distributed leadership is the idea that leadership is not the preserve of an individual but is a fluid or emergent property rather than a fixed phenomenon" (Harris 2008, 4). The fluid nature of distributed leadership indicates that it is a response to changes in the internal and external environments, which is the type of leadership learning environment that can sustain graduates' effective practice.

3. A Curriculum That is Empowering

After examining a number of definitions, the one that comes closest to how we view curriculum defines it as "…a desired goal or set of values that can be activated through a development process, culminating in experiences for learners" (Wiles and Bondi 2015, 3). This definition considers curriculum content, environment, experiences, values, teaching and learning. This definition qualifies curriculum as a developmental process, giving the impression that having experienced the curriculum, some personal and professional growth should take place. It therefore puts the focus on the interactions: social, psychological, cultural, academic, physical, historical, ideological and spiritual that take place within a "learning environment" geared towards achieving stated and specific goals and promoting specific values. The learning environment is not a bounded space. In this regard, the curriculum is an environment created to develop particular goals and values in those who experience the space. The goals can be defined in terms of academic content, skills, dispositions, attitudes, cognitive, affective, well-being and psychomotor.

4. Continuing Professional Learning That is Empowering and Inspiring

Jones (2021) states that "professional learning involves active learning; it is a continuing process; it focuses on enquiry, analysis, reflection, evaluation, further action; it should be professionally critical; in its best forms, it is collaborative; and it enables an approach which is not confined to a linear interpretation of future events and ways of working" (2). We accept the continuing professional learning process expressed by Jones (2021) as the most suitable for sustaining graduates' effective practice and offer it for use with this model. However, we also bear in mind that the human element of any organization will always present challenges to institutional functioning. Thus, we consider that informal learning through professional and personal examples can also empower and inspire practitioners to strive for the goal of sculpting their best selves through self-awareness that leads to conscious positive transformation (Yamin-Ali 2021).

5. A Context That Supports Learning

A supportive learning context must be equipped with sufficient infrastructure that meets the physical, social, emotional and well-being needs of the learning community. Thus, on the physical side, schools should have the resources, for example, internet connections, clean classrooms, outdoor seating areas, and teaching and learning materials that staff need to function. In terms of social and emotional infrastructure, we advocate that in creating a context and culture of innovation in schools such that graduates of professional learning programmes can sustain their practice, schools consider the OECD (2017) seven learning principles as follows:

1. The learning environment recognizes the learners as its core participants, encourages their active engagement and develops in them an understanding of their own activity as learners.

2. The learning environment is founded on the social nature of learning and actively encourages well-organized co-operative learning.
3. The learning professionals within the learning environment are highly attuned to the learners' motivations and the key role of emotions in achievement.
4. The learning environment is acutely sensitive to the individual differences among the learners in it, including their prior knowledge.
5. The learning environment devises programmes that demand hard work and challenge from all without excessive overload.
6. The learning environment operates with clarity of expectations and deploys assessment strategies consistent with these expectations; there is strong emphasis on formative feedback to support learning.
7. The learning environment strongly promotes "horizontal connectedness" across areas of knowledge and subjects as well as to the community and the wider world (22–25).

Additionally, schools should have access to medical facilities to address the needs of its community. This might include having a nurse on site or on call and with regard to meeting the mental needs of the community, schools should also have social workers on site or on call.

6. A Culture of Research

Research is a critical driver in raising the quality of teaching and learning at schools and is also an integral part of most initial or in-service teacher preparation programmes. Most teacher preparation programmes expose their participants to the skills and knowledge of conducting action research. Nevertheless, once teachers complete these programmes, little or no research is conducted for many reasons, including that the culture and context do not support teacher research (James and Augustin

2017). We advocate that schools not only facilitate teacher classroom action research (Herbert and Rainford 2014), but also do broader research that can inform the improvement and change agenda in the school.

7. A Culture of Collaboration and Establishing Partnerships

Collaboration is a process and a product innovation; thus, it is a means and an end (James and Figaro-Henry 2017; Herbert, Rampersad and George 2009). Therefore, while collaboration may start with dialogue, it should end with action and tangible outcomes. However, it is not sufficient to foster a collaborative environment with stakeholders within the learning environment; it is equally important to establish partnerships. Schleicher (2015) states that innovation is now more than before the product of partnerships: how we share, process and connect knowledge. Partnerships are formed where two persons or groups agree to work together to achieve mutual goals. For example, there can be school and parents' partnerships, school and business community partnerships and professional partnerships. Partnerships can be formal and informal, and both are encouraged to sustain graduates' effective practice in schools.

Recommendations

This study was situated in a local context and as such the recommendations that follow will naturally speak to this specific context. Nevertheless, the writers acknowledge that given the global nature of the issue, the recommendations proffered have implications for not just the singular context within which the research was done, but for a wider global context.

a. How the SoE Sees Its Role in CPD and CPL to Help Teachers Better Deal with Their Liminality

We suggest that the SoE should create professional learning activities and opportunities for graduates to buttress their skills, knowledge and dispositions post initial preparation programmes. In this way, the SoE will foster CPL and CPD to allow graduates to be predictive in the socially dynamic environment in which they operate.

b. How the SoE Sees Its Role in Influencing Wider Culture

The SoE should foster partnership agreements with schools, through the MoE, to facilitate school improvement. For example, it can organize activities that provide the opportunities for shared learning that enhances school improvement. Additionally, the SoE can work with school leaders to drive on-site continuing professional learning activities appropriate to their contexts to build capacity, create learning communities to enhance collaboration and initiate a variety of learning experiences. Learning communities should also extend to other schools and districts or even be country-wide through the coordination of either subject associations, or more formally through the Curriculum Division of the MoE.

c. Bridging the Gap among the SoE and Stakeholders in the Drive toward Effective Practice

Perhaps the SoE should take stronger and more definitive steps towards continuing meaningful dialogue with the MoE with an aim of making bilateral decisions concerning educational issues. It should position itself as an initiator of discussions, not only with the MoE, but with formal bodies such as principals' associations and teachers' associations, and with other stakeholders, such as parents, students and the general public, as an equal partner in determining the direction of teaching and learning in schools.

d. Policy Change

The MoE should institute a policy which stipulates that promotion to positions of middle and senior management in schools should require qualifications in both educational administration and in subject specialization. In particular, the educational administration qualification should be at the master's level. Furthermore, there should be formal avenues for those who are not in those positions but possess the educational administration qualification to utilize their specialized skills and knowledge within the school, perhaps through a formally constituted management team with the requisite remuneration. Such a team, of course, will function within established terms of reference.

Further, the MoE should review its entry requirements for teaching, which should be an undergraduate degree in a subject area, in addition to pre-service teacher preparation. That teacher preparation programme must include a practicum. Such pre-service preparation must be linked to a licensure system, which is based on continuing professional learning.

e. Research

We recommend schools engage in their own research to build upon this research on the role of culture and context as it impacts their professional realities. The SoE stands ready and willing to partner with schools to support their research efforts.

f. SoE's Response to Perceptions of Misalignment between Programme Content and Specific School Contexts

SoE DipEd staff should develop a communication strategy that will continually remind students that the content of the in-service DipEd programme is contextually relevant, as opportunities for authentic learning within the practice context are provided. The Action Research Project requires students to identify a problem within their contexts and design an intervention. The practicum provides opportunities for practice in context. In addition, to strengthen programme relevance, SoE staff should request student input in identifying issues to be explored during the programme in order to improve the quality of teaching and learning at their schools.

Concluding Remarks

Contemporary thinking about the purpose of education is that it is a vehicle for holistic development of students who can think critically and creatively, solve problems, work collaboratively with diverse groups and communicate effectively for the development of human societies (OECD 2017; Harris and Jones 2017; James and Figaro-Henry 2017; Hattie 2012). Professional learning programmes should aim to introduce educators to new perspectives on education and foster teacher transformation. Such programmes should also encourage and support participants in their attempts to operationalize the theories and principles presented. However, upon graduation, the participant is not the only factor in sustaining change and is within a liminal space with the potential for deep-seated transformation, which is related to the environment in which he/she functions.

The mediating factors within a school's context and culture determine the extent to which the professional learning experiences are sustained in the graduates' practice context. These factors can be both positive and negative. Where the school culture and context are revealed to be supportive of the DipEd theories and principles, there is a higher degree of sustainability of DipEd practice, and the converse also applies. The participants in this study have all said that it can be difficult but not impossible to implement changes within their various contexts and have provided evidence of sustainability, not just as maintaining practices to which they were exposed but also by their disposition for continuous learning and improvement. It is instructive that the main reasons suggested for reduced application of principles and theories are infrastructural (physical structure of the plant, amenities and resources) and also workload, time constraints, student push-back and lack of support from colleagues and administrative policies. It therefore behoves the programme developers to advocate that at levels above the school – the district level, the central MoE – the facilitating factors, such as leadership support (principal and middle management) and development of learning communities, as reported in this study, be adopted where necessary and strengthened as required. The inhibiting factors identified should be further explored with stakeholders, to develop deeper understandings which can lead to joint solutions that can redound to the benefit of all.

Discussions in this book revolved around the factors that facilitated and hindered teachers' effective practice in their school contexts five years after they graduated from initial professional teacher preparation in one setting. Apart from practice in their classroom, there was a focus on how these graduates contributed to their schools' development. The six chapters explored to what extent and in what ways culture and context impacted this practice. The findings we have presented support the idea that culture and context do matter in the professional practice of educators who have had the benefit of professional learning. The cases presented in this book reveal a reality where professionally prepared educators seem to possess the knowledge, skills and dispositions to function effectively but need both internal and external support, not just to remain professionally buoyant but to soar as they attempt to make a positive difference in their students' lives and their school community. This book also acknowledges the significant role of tertiary teacher education institutions in consistently ensuring a fit between learning and development opportunities and the professional needs of schoolteachers and leaders, as perceived/evident in their actual professional contexts. This supports Varela and Maxwell's (2015) conclusion that improvements to teacher preparation lie in a programme's ability to develop the graduate as an adaptable, responsive and lifelong learner. Hopefully, this book provides a starting point for the consideration of such a fit.

References

Cilliers, Jacobus, Brahm Fleisch, Janeli Kotzé, Mpumi Mohohlwane, and Stephen Taylor. 2020. 'The Challenge of Sustaining Effective Teaching: Spillovers, Fade-Out, and the Cost-Effectiveness of Teacher Development Programs.' Working paper. Department of Basic Education. Pretoria, South Africa. https://custom.cvent.com/4E741122FD8B4A1 B97E483EC8BB51CC4/files/thechallengeofsustainingeffectiveteachingwithteaching with appendix.pdf.

Darling-Hammond, Linda, Lisa Flook, Channa Cook-Harvey, Brigid Barron, and David Osher. 2020. "Implications for Educational Practice of the Science of Learning and Development." *Applied Developmental Science* 24 (2): 97–140. https://doi.org/10.1080/10888691.2018.1537791.

Hammerness, Karen, Linda Darling-Hammond, and John Bransford. 2005. "How Teachers Learn and Develop." In *Preparing Teachers for a Changing World: What Teachers Should Learn and Be Able to Do*, edited by Linda Darling-Hammond and John Bransford, 358–89. San Francisco, CA: Jossey-Bass.

Harris, Alma. 2008. "Distributed Leadership: According to the Evidence." *Journal of Educational Administration* 46 (2): 172–88. https://doi.org/10.1108/09578230810863253.

———, and Michelle Jones. 2017. "Leading Professional Learning: Putting Teachers at the Centre." *School Leadership & Management* 37 (4): 331–33. https://doi.org/10.1080/13632434.2017.1343705.

Hattie, John. 2012. *Visible Learning for Teachers: Maximising Impact on Teachers*. London: Routledge.

Herbert, Susan, and Marcia Rainford. 2014. "Developing a Model for Continuous Professional Development by Action Research." *Professional Development in Education* 40 (2): 243–64.

———, Joycelyn Rampersad, and June George. 2009. "Collaborating to Reform Science Education in Context: Issues, Challenges, and Benefits." *Caribbean Curriculum* 16 (1): 17–39.

James, Freddy, and Désirée Augustin. 2017. "Improving Teachers' Pedagogical and Instructional Practice through Action Research: Potential and Problems." *Educational Action Research* 26 (2): 333–48. https://doi.org/10.1080/09650792.2017.1332655.

———, and Sandra Figaro-Henry. 2017. "Building Collective Leadership Capacity Using Twenty-First Century Digital Tools." *School Leadership and Management Journal* 37 (5): 520–36. https://doi.org/10.1080/13632434.2017.1367277.

Jones, Ken. 2021. "'Professional Development' or 'Professional Learning' ... and Does It Matter?" Education Workforce Council. Accessed May 21, 2021. https://www.ewc.wales/site/index.php/en/about /staff-room/son-archive/43-english/about/staff-room/blog-archive /93-ken-jones-professional-development-or-professional-learning-and-does-it-matter.html.

OECD (Organisation for Economic Co-operation and Development). 2017. *The OECD Handbook for Innovative Learning Environments*. Paris: OECD Publishing.

Schleicher, Andreas. 2015. "Foreword" to *Schooling Redesigned: Towards Innovative Learning Systems* by the Organisation for Economic Co-operation and Development (OECD), 3–5. Paris: OECD Publishing.

Sheninger, Eric C., and Thomas C. Murray. 2017. *Learning Transformed: 8 Keys to Designing Tomorrow's Schools, Today*. Alexandria, VA: Association of Supervision and Curriculum Development (ASCD).

Varela, Daniella G., and Gerri M. Maxwell. 2015. "Effectiveness of Teacher Training: Voices of Teachers Serving High-Needs Populations of Students." *Journal of Case Studies in Education* 7. https://files.eric.ed.gov/fulltext/EJ1117610.pdf.

Wiles, Jon W., and Joseph C. Bondi. 2015. *Curriculum Development: A Guide to Practice*. 9th ed. Boston, MA: Pearson.

Yamin-Ali, Jennifer. 2014. *Data-Driven Decision-Making in Schools: Lessons from Trinidad*. New York: Palgrave Macmillan.

———. 2021. *Teacher Educator Experiences and Professional Development: Perspectives from the Caribbean*. New York: Palgrave Macmillan.

Index

21st century skills, 28
Active learning strategies, 71
ACTT, 15
Administrative, 41, 143, 157–59, 162, 169, 180
Analogies, 65
Apprenticeship of observation, 8
Authentic assessment, 125
Availability of technology, 84, 122

Belonging, 13, 140
Big ideas in science, 132
Blended-learning, 156–57
Bloom's Taxonomy, 61–62, 66, 68, 101

Capacity Building, 18
CARICOM, 15
Case, 4, 8, 9–10, 22–23, 25, 36, 47–48, 50–51, 54, 64, 68, 79, 88–89, 106, 116, 118, 121, 135, 138, 143, 145, 156, 163, 170

Challenges, 5, 10, 12, 28, 107, 110, 164, 181
Challenging, 10
Change agent, 136, 163
Classroom, 4, 10–13, 17, 19, 23–24, 35, 43–47, 49–52, 55, 59, 62–64, 69, 81–83, 85, 86, 92, 94, 99, 113, 116–18, 125, 127, 143–44, 147, 150, 158, 162–63, 176, 180
Management, 24, 50–51, 62, 92
Clinical supervision, 36, 93, 94, 134, 142, 143
Co-Curricular, 148
Cognitive flexibility, 8, 72
Collaboration, 4, 18, 21, 39, 51, 72, 77, 81– 82, 96–97, 148, 155–56, 161, 167, 172, 176–77
Collaborative, 3, 10, 17, 20, 47, 84, 96, 147, 164, 167, 171, 174, 176
Effort, 84, 147
Model, 10

Commitment to learning, 85, 88, 90
Committee, 143, 159
Community of practice, 9, 105, 140, 156, 160
Competencies, 4, 13–14, 19, 24, 37, 65, 98, 102, 166
Concept maps, 59
Concepts, 2, 4, 13, 19, 47, 57–58, 61, 64–65, 131–32, 136
Confidence, 48, 97–98, 131, 149, 167
Connectedness, 140, 164, 175
Constructivist, 13, 46
Contextual, 10–13, 17, 26, 106, 110, 114, 135–36, 138, 167
Continuing professional learning, 17–18, 20, 72–73, 79, 138, 172, 174, 177–78
Contribution, 5, 10, 13, 27, 140, 147, 152
Cross-case analysis, 25
Cultural, 6, 10–11, 14, 17, 20, 26, 39, 89, 103, 106, 110, 114, 136, 138, 143, 151, 167, 173
Culture of innovation, 7, 12, 172, 174
Curriculum, 17–18, 22, 24, 36, 53, 84, 86–87, 89, 105–6, 119, 124, 129, 143, 147, 150, 160, 169, 172–73

Data collection, 9, 23
Decision-making, 69, 119, 153
Deep learning, 5, 58, 72–73
Denominational, 43, 121
Departments, 2, 6, 15, 20, 23, 36, 40–41, 84, 92, 105, 120, 145, 163, 168
Development, 2, 5, 10, 13, 26–32, 74, 78, 93–94, 107–9, 139–41, 157, 165, 181–82
Differentiation, 69
Diped programme, 2, 11, 17, 24, 33–34, 38–41, 45, 48–49, 51, 53, 55, 60–65, 67–68, 73, 76–79, 81–84, 89, 91, 93–97, 99–101, 104–7, 111–13, 117, 120, 122, 124–27, 130–34, 136–38, 147–48, 154, 164, 167, 178
Dispositions, 2, 4, 13, 20, 110, 130, 154, 173, 177, 180
Distributed leadership, 173

Educational
 change, 28, 29, 107
 division, 36, 112
 psychology, 157
 administration, 2, 4, 22–23, 33, 41, 72–73, 79, 105, 138, 168, 170, 178
Effective schools, 163
Efficacy, 7, 12, 37, 58, 73, 98, 131, 167
Empirical, 10, 170
Empirically, 10
Encouragement by administration, 83, 90
Engagement, 11–12, 21, 63, 65, 69, 95, 100, 172, 174
Environments, 2, 10, 12, 19, 69, 78, 105, 173
Ethos, 50
Evidence-based, 9–10, 13, 15

Extra-curricular, 132, 151

Factors
  external, 12, 89, 101, 103, 106, 133, 169
  facilitating, 12, 105-6, 167, 180
  inhibiting, 113, 126, 180
  personal, 12, 78, 85, 105-6
Flipped classroom, 59
Foreign language, 2, 22, 39, 48-49, 53, 55, 81, 83-86, 88, 91, 118, 121, 137, 147-49, 153, 163, 169-70
Formal curriculum, 43, 86, 88
Functioning department, 84, 90

Generic culture, 17, 79, 103, 114, 121, 134- 35, 138, 145, 154
Goals, 6, 17, 20, 173, 176
Group work, 24, 47, 49, 62, 71, 127, 158
Guided inquiry, 64

Horizontal connectedness, 175

ICT policy, 93, 106, 124
Implementation, 3, 5, 24, 70, 78, 91-93, 105-6, 157, 159
Inductive reasoning, 64-65
Influence, 9-12, 17, 26, 35, 60, 73, 76, 82, 101, 103, 106-7, 125, 132, 136-37, 146-48, 152
Infrastructure, 77
  physical, 113
  technological, 113
Initial teacher education, 9
Innovation, 7, 12, 21-22, 106, 167, 174, 176

Innovative, 10, 152, 168, 170, 172
In-service, 4, 10, 17, 13-14, 18, 76, 175, 178
Instructional leadership, 20, 172
Instructional triangle, 7, 11
Insufficient space, 127
Interaction, 4, 11, 59, 70-71, 142, 156-58
Interactive instruction, 49

Jigsaw, 58, 62, 100-101

Lab demonstration, 97
Lab space, 97
Laboratory technician, 97, 126
Lack of support, 180
Leadership, 3, 5-6, 16, 20-21, 40, 41, 69, 73, 77-79, 91-92, 97, 102-103, 105, 112, 115, 137-38, 143, 145, 154-55, 158, 161, 163-64, 168, 170-73, 180
  roles, 158
Learning
  context, 13, 33, 59-60, 72, 88, 107, 163, 166, 174
  environment, 9, 17, 41, 55, 69, 79, 89-90, 93, 115, 121, 134, 137, 154, 161, 163, 172-76
Lesson planning, 35, 39, 50, 61, 89, 93, 100, 132, 148, 158
Licensure, 18, 178
Lifelong
  learners, 9-10, 34, 36
  learning, 10, 73, 99, 106, 142
Liminal space, 14, 166-67, 179
Liminality, 177
Linguistic proficiency, 147
Literacy challenges, 50, 120

Meaningful learning, 96, 133
Mentors, 2, 6, 11, 13
Mentorship, 40, 93, 112, 144–45, 155, 163
Metacognition, 14, 141, 156, 160
Methodology, 11
Micro-political, 16
Middle management, 91, 142–43, 158, 167, 169, 180
Misalignment, 178
Model, 5, 7, 10, 13, 30–31, 74, 108, 139, 165–66, 170–71, 181
Multi-site, 9, 22

Negotiation, 11, 33, 157
Networking, 39
Networks, 4, 21
New strategies, 59, 99, 129, 138, 154
Non-academic, 51
Novice teachers, 34, 41, 144

Observation data, 24
Organizational
  conditions, 141
  structure, 16, 79, 91, 145

Parental impact, 101
Partnerships, 6, 172, 176
Passion for teaching, 85, 90
Perceived culture, 17, 90, 154
Personal beliefs and characteristics, 85
Policy change, 178
Practical work, 64–65, 69, 97, 105, 125–29, 158
Practice, 2–15, 17, 19–22, 24–25, 33–39, 44–49, 51, 53–55, 59–63, 67, 71–73, 76–79, 81, 83–85, 87–95, 99–100, 102, 104–5, 107, 110–11, 113–14, 117–18, 120–21, 124–25, 132, 134–39, 145, 152, 154, 156, 159–60, 163–64, 166–74, 176, 178–80
  space, 7, 10, 172
  context, 6, 9, 33, 59–60, 63, 67, 71–72, 104–5, 111, 136, 163, 169, 178–79
Preparation
  initial, 9, 11, 73, 177
Prior learning, 13
Problem of complexity, 8
Problem of enactment, 8
Problem-solving, 14, 58, 169
Professional
  capital, 27
  development, 12–14, 17–18, 92–93
  identity, 162
  learning, 2–4, 6–7, 9–14, 18, 20–22, 36–37, 40–41, 72–73, 79, 92–93, 103, 105–7, 110–11, 114, 127, 136, 138, 140–42, 145–46, 150, 156, 163, 166–70, 172, 174, 177–80
  practice, 2, 14, 138, 166, 180
  learning communities, 11
  orientation, 17, 40, 55, 79, 90, 102–3, 134, 137, 153
Programme, 2, 4–8, 9–12, 13–14, 17–19, 22–24, 33, 35–37, 41, 43–44, 48, 52, 60, 64, 67, 76–79, 81–82, 84, 89–90, 92–94, 98, 100, 103–4, 106–7, 111–12, 119,

127, 130–33, 138, 140–43, 151–52, 154, 164, 166–70, 178–81
providers, 76
relevance, 106, 179
sponsors, 76
Provider, 33, 73
Psychomotor, 145, 173

Qualitative, 9, 22
Quality, 6, 10, 14–15, 17, 20, 41, 55, 61, 69, 70, 73, 75, 79, 90, 115, 121, 134, 135, 137–38, 145, 148–49, 153–54, 159, 161, 163, 175, 179
Questioning, 24, 36, 45, 64, 66–69, 71, 100–101

Reflection, 3, 8, 9, 35, 42, 54, 56, 63–64, 67, 71, 80, 88, 90, 99, 103–4, 115, 122, 136, 146, 154, 162, 170, 172, 174
Reflective, 17, 35, 63, 69, 99
Reform, 181
Research, 2–4, 9–11, 13, 17–19, 21–23, 25–26, 36–37, 47, 53–54, 57–59, 63, 68, 72, 76, 78, 81, 85, 92, 112–13, 118, 130, 142–43, 158, 160–61, 164, 167, 171, 175–76, 178
Resources, 10–13, 47, 52, 60–61, 68–69, 89, 101, 104–6, 117, 124–26, 148–49, 152, 154, 156, 158–59, 162–63, 169–70, 174, 180
  human, 12, 118
  lack of, 38, 126
  material, 12
  teaching, 148
Role-playing, 35, 86

School
  climate, 155
  community, 20, 145, 153, 180
  context, 7, 9, 13–14, 24, 50–51, 148, 166, 167
  contexts, 22, 41, 76, 135, 180
  culture, 9, 12, 16–17, 25, 55, 69, 72, 77–79, 102, 106, 111, 121, 125, 134, 137, 139, 144, 151, 153, 161, 168–69, 179
  development, 13, 23, 140, 141, 148–50, 151–53, 157–59, 161–62, 166, 168
  factors, 12, 77, 83, 91, 105, 112
  improvement, 26, 29–32, 74, 108, 139, 165
  leadership, 12, 20, 91, 104, 141
  policy, 113, 142
  resources, 97, 104, 125
  success, 111, 169
  system, 13
  systems, 20
School Based Assessment, 37, 65, 144, 168
School-based practices, 118
Science, 2, 11, 22–23, 33, 35, 57–58, 60–61, 64–72, 91–92, 95–98, 102, 104–5, 112–14, 126–28, 132, 134, 137–38, 142–45, 157–58, 161–63, 170
  activities, 96
  curriculum, 66, 97, 145
  fair, 96–97
  labs, 113–14

Self-efficacy, 58, 73, 131
Situated learning, 9
Social, 26, 32, 109
Social factors, 55
Socio-economic, 12, 24, 101, 110, 121, 138
Staff development, 28
Stakeholder
 external, 144
 perspectives, 2
 relationships, 144
Standards, 14-15, 95
Stories, 15, 25-26
Strategies, 4, 6-7, 12, 23, 25, 35, 43, 54, 58, 59, 62, 64-65, 67, 71, 77, 82, 95, 98-101, 113, 124, 126, 128-31, 133, 138, 148, 152, 154, 159, 167, 170, 175
Student
 achievement, 12-13, 16, 21, 135, 145, 161, 164
 culture, 12, 120-21
 empowerment, 22, 72
 factors, 98, 104, 114, 130, 131
 performance, 99, 103, 156-58, 160
Student-centred, 17, 22, 35, 47, 55, 57, 60, 64, 69-72, 79, 81-82, 85, 98, 101-3, 117, 121, 124, 126-28, 131, 133-35, 137, 154, 170
Student-centred strategies, 98, 124, 128, 131
Supervision, 4, 24, 34, 36-38, 40, 61, 73, 77, 78, 92-94, 103, 112, 115, 118, 121, 134, 142-45, 163, 168

Support, 2, 4-5, 9, 16, 20, 33, 47, 51-52, 63, 76, 83, 86, 89-90, 95, 97, 101, 103-6, 111, 119-20, 125-26, 136, 138, 144-45, 159, 161-63, 167-69, 175, 178-80
Sustain, 3, 6, 11-12, 83, 85, 89-91, 98-99, 107, 120-21, 138, 168-70, 172-74, 176
Sustainability, 5-6, 8-9, 10-11, 21, 59, 76, 102, 104, 106-7, 110-11, 125, 134, 138- 39, 169-70, 179
Sustaining effective practice, 12-14, 18-19, 89, 103, 107, 120, 137-38, 166
Syllabus coverage, 129, 136
System improvement, 3, 141
Systemic factors, 111

Teacher
 autonomy, 168
 commitment, 75, 140
 development, 9
 education, 5, 8-10, 12, 17, 14, 18, 19, 104, 110, 140, 180
 factors, 98, 104, 131
 preparation, 8-9, 14, 18, 21, 111, 138, 175, 178, 180-81
 quality, 145
Teacher-centred, 64
Teacher-directed, 69-70
Teachers' belief, 6, 12
Teachers' beliefs and characteristics, 99
Teachers' characteristics, 13, 131
Teachers' lack of cooperation, 119
Teaching philosophy, 5, 55, 154

Team
 teaching, 167
 teamwork, 140
Technology, 31–32, 52, 68, 74, 84, 92–93, 116
Time, 3, 6, 9, 13–15, 17–18, 21, 35, 38, 40, 47– 49, 57–58, 62–63, 65–67, 82, 84–85, 88, 92–93, 96, 101, 112, 114, 117–19, 126–31, 137, 142, 144, 149, 151–52, 156–57, 160, 164, 167, 180
Tradition, 21, 152
Trainee locus of control, 75
Trainee motivation, 75
Training outcomes, 75
Training workshops, 143
Transfer, 5, 7–8, 10–12, 26, 31, 33, 44, 59, 75, 107–8
 knowledge, 7, 172
 of knowledge, 5, 10–11, 13, 33, 59, 103, 105, 136, 166
 of learning, 5, 9–10, 12, 31, 55, 72, 75–77, 111, 169
 of skills, 75
 process, 75
Transferring professional learning, 1, 3
Transformation, 3, 14, 11, 60, 166–67, 174, 179
Transitioning, 9, 17

Uncooperative Department, 119, 121
Unique culture, 17, 41, 90, 154
Unwilling colleagues, 119

Values, 17, 20, 35, 43, 87, 90, 110, 125, 133–34, 136, 138, 173
Visible learning, 141
Vision, 17, 20, 85, 103, 138, 154, 164, 168, 172

Well-being, 143, 145, 173–74
Wider culture, 17, 41, 55, 103, 114, 121, 135, 138, 146

www.ingramcontent.com/pod-product-compliance
Lightning Source LLC
Chambersburg PA
CBHW030826230426
43667CB00008B/1402